HOW TO SUCCESSFULLY TRANSITION STUDENTS INTO COLLEGE

Challenging traditional notions about why successful high school graduates struggle in college, this book sheds light on the obstacles that hinder a seamless transition and provides clear guidance on how to overcome them.

Drawing from research and real-life stories of educators and students across a variety of institutions, Geddes illuminates a critical truth: it's the successes students had in high school that work against them in college, not their failures. This book explores the hidden structural, functional, and cognitive traps that undermine students' academic work, strain teacher-student relationships, and impose artificial limits on their potential. Armed with formulas for academic success, it provides tools for guiding students towards levels of high performance and supplies teaching methods for how to create an educational environment conducive to success.

Packed with practical advice, actionable steps, and inspiring success stories, this landmark book serves as an invaluable roadmap for college educators seeking to empower their students and revolutionize their institutions.

Leonard Geddes is the founder of The LearnWell Projects, an academic success organization devoted to making learning more visible, manageable, and effective. A highly regarded higher education consultant and strategist with 20+ years' experience, he is also the former Associate Dean of Students and Director of the Learning Commons at Lenoir-Rhyne University, USA.

HOW TO SUCCESSFULLY TRANSITION STUDENTS INTO COLLEGE

From Traps to Triumph

Leonard Geddes

Routledge
Taylor & Francis Group

NEW YORK AND LONDON

Designed cover image: © Lizbe Coetzee

First published 2024
by Routledge
605 Third Avenue, New York, NY 10158

and by Routledge
4 Park Square, Milton Park, Abingdon, Oxon, OX14 4RN

Routledge is an imprint of the Taylor & Francis Group, an informa business

© 2024 Leonard Geddes

ISBN: 978-1-642-67288-6 (hbk)
ISBN: 978-1-642-67289-3 (pbk)
ISBN: 978-1-003-44725-2 (ebk)

DOI: 10.4324/9781003447252

Typeset in Galliard
by codeMantra

CONTENTS

SECTION III
Cognitive Traps 121

PREFACE

On July 4th, 2019, my family was staying with our extended families in a beachfront house on Kure Beach, a small town off the North Carolina coast. We had been renting the house for the Independence Day holiday for the past five years, as a way of reconnecting the families.

On that fateful day, as I watched the relentless battle between swimmers and rip currents unfold before my eyes, little did I know that it would become a profound metaphor for the challenges students face when transitioning into college. The events I witnessed on that beach in Kure Beach, North Carolina, opened my eyes to the hidden dangers that lurk beneath the surface of seemingly calm waters.

As the day unfolded, lifeguards valiantly rescued thirteen swimmers caught in rip currents, each struggling to escape the powerful grip of the tides. It was a staggering sight—a constant stream of unsuspecting families falling prey to the same perilous mistake. I couldn't help but wonder why this particular day had witnessed such an alarming number of near-disasters.

The beachgoers were well aware of the dangers, with red flags raised to signal the rough seas. Parents cautioned their children to stay close to the shore, and adults themselves exercised caution. Yet, every half an hour or so, someone would find themselves in distress, and lifeguards would leap into action to save them.

I was initially puzzled by this recurring pattern. How could so many swimmers, aware of the danger, willingly plunge into the rip currents? The answer came to me as I delved deeper into the nature of these currents— they possessed a deceptive allure that entranced unsuspecting beachgoers.

A clear sequence emerged: First, swimmers were lured by the rip currents' seemingly placid entry points, mistaking them for safe passages amidst the crashing waves. Then, they believed they could swim their way out of the current's grasp, only to exhaust themselves in futile attempts. Finally, the lifeguards would step in to save them. And as one family moved on, another would unknowingly walk the same path.

This pattern echoed the challenges faced by students in higher education. Just as swimmers fell into the rip currents' clutches, students too found themselves ensnared in transition traps that disrupted and derailed their academic journeys.

The Lure

The allure of the rip current lies in the calm facade it presents to those seeking to enter the water. Similarly, new college students are drawn towards transition traps in their quest for a smooth entry into the realm of higher education. They unwittingly rely on familiar approaches from their high school days, believing these methods to be safe and suitable. Yet, these seemingly comfortable practices set them on a path of academic underperformance.

The Deception

Escaping a rip current is a relatively straightforward process—swimmers need only swim parallel to the shore for a short distance before redirecting their course back to land. However, most people only realize they are trapped when the current has already pulled them farther from safety. Panic sets in, and the instinct to swim against the current and save oneself takes over. But even the most skilled swimmers are unlikely to overcome the force of the rip tide. In a similar fashion, students caught in transition traps often redouble their efforts, unaware that their exertions will prove ultimately futile.

The Delay

Another parallel emerges in the delay that swimmers and students face when seeking help. Swimmers, initially unaware of their predicament, hesitate to alert others of their distress. Time slips away, and with each passing moment, their energy wanes, leaving them sinking and without the strength to fight any longer. Similarly, students caught in transition traps often wait far too long before reaching out for assistance. This tendency is especially pronounced among advanced swimmers and high-achieving students, who frequently resist seeking help longer than their peers.

The Rescue

But just as lifeguards are trained to identify rip currents and recognize distress signals, educators can play a pivotal role in identifying students caught in transition traps. By equipping yourself with the knowledge and tools to navigate these challenges, you can create environments that are free from transition traps and empower your students to thrive.

Throughout my career, I have had the privilege of training numerous college and university educators to identify the signs of students struggling with transition traps. Their stories, along with the stories of the students they have helped, are now presented within these pages. Through their insights, tools, and actionable takeaways, you too can create an environment that ensures a successful transition for students into college.

The journey ahead explores the depths of these transition traps, unearthing the strategies to avoid them and highlighting the transformative power of early intervention. Together, let us navigate the treacherous waters of the transition into college and pave the way for student success.

ACKNOWLEDGMENTS

I would like to express my deepest gratitude to my wife Cindy and our children, Cassidy and Brandon, for their unwavering support throughout this project. Their understanding, patience, and encouragement have been instrumental in allowing me the necessary space and time to bring this book to fruition.

I am also grateful to my extended family, friends, and colleagues who have been understanding and supportive during this intensive period of focus. Your understanding and encouragement have meant the world to me.

Lastly, I would like to extend my heartfelt thanks to the educators, students, and institutions who placed their trust in me to address their challenges and share their stories. Your invaluable contributions and encouragement have inspired me to write this book and have greatly enriched its content.

Thank you all for your enduring support, understanding, and belief in the importance of improving student performance and successfully transitioning students into college.

1

INTRODUCTION

Imagine a world where students seamlessly transition from high school to college, equipped with the skills and mindset needed to excel academically. In this world, students would effortlessly navigate the path from high school to college, armed with the tools and mindset essential for academic excellence, thus transforming the educational landscape. These students would seamlessly apply the perspectives and practices honed in high school, propelling them to continued success in college. The standards of tests and assessments would remain demanding, yet the rates of D, F, and W grades would plummet. First-generation students and students of color would thrive in science and math courses, defying the notion of being diverted to "easier" programs. Teachers would be fueled by pride in their profession, fostering an unwavering sense of satisfaction. The public would rekindle their reverence for education, particularly higher education. Alas, this idyllic vision remains elusive. Instead, students often find themselves trapped in the limbo between the familiar territory of high school triumphs and the uncharted challenges of college life. This book embarks on a journey to illuminate the academic transition traps that impede students' progress and to unveil how colleges and universities can empower them to overcome these barriers. By unearthing the truth behind student underperformance, we can dismantle the misconceptions and narratives that constrain their academic success. With a profound understanding of these challenges, we can forge a new path towards liberation and open the doors to limitless possibilities for our students.

Believe it or not, your students are pretty good at doing academic work. Consider the staggering amount of time students invest in academic work

DOI: 10.4324/9781003447252-1

before entering college. By the time they step foot on campus, the average student has devoted over 16,000 hours to their education, excluding any additional work done outside of school. This calculation, derived from seven to eight hours of school per day for 180 days a year over thirteen years, highlights the immense potential and readiness students bring with them. Additionally, with only 66% of students immediately entering college after high school graduation, we are working with the cream of the crop (Immediate College Enrollment Rate: NCES, 2022). However, the disheartening truth is that approximately 63% of college students fail to graduate (Undergraduate Retention and Graduation Rates: National Center for Educational Statistics, 2022). Clearly, something about the college academic environment is impeding the success of these promising individuals.

As a college educator, you witness firsthand the challenges of student underperformance. Balancing administrative reports of enrolling better students with the harsh reality of continued low performance can be disheartening. It is tempting to believe that your students lack intelligence or work ethic. Settling on this conclusion is reasonable. How else can you reconcile the chasm that exists between students' expected performance and their actual performance? The disconnect between their expected performance and actual outcomes can leave you questioning whether they are lying about how much they study or if there is an underlying trickery involved. And when instructional enhancements—such as test guides, study maps, recitation sessions, and reteaching material—don't sufficiently boost students' performance, we firmly conclude that our students are broken. However, the truth is: our students are not broken, they are stuck in limbo, between what worked for them in the past and what is needed in the present. This book aims to unearth that truth, liberating students, teachers, and institutions from the constraints of misperceptions and negative narratives that hinder academic success.

Recognizing the persistent problem of underperformance, many educators turn to various forms of professional development. They enhance their content, modify their teaching methods, and experiment with different assessments. While these efforts may initially feel like progress, they often fall short of producing the transformative enhancements expected. It is at this juncture that we might attribute students' struggles to brain drain from excessive screen time or assume that the pandemic has permanently damaged their abilities. Blaming the high school education system is also a common response. However, these cognitive distortions do not offer practical solutions.

Let me introduce a more hopeful reality: our students are not irreparably broken or inherently apathetic. They are trapped—caught in a web of transitional dilemmas that have yet to be comprehensively addressed.

This book endeavors to identify these transition traps, which arise from the intricate dynamics between relationships and transitions. By understanding these dynamics, we can unveil solutions that empower students to navigate the college academic landscape successfully.

Throughout students' precollege years, they develop three fundamental relationships: (1) a relationship with the environment in which they learned, (2) a relationship with the educators who teach them, and (3) a relationship with the work they undertake. These relationships form the bedrock of their academic infrastructure, shaping *how they learn* and *what they learn*. This book synthesizes real stories and research to compare how students leverage these relationships for success in high school versus college. It makes it evident that new college students are ensnared by their past triumphs rather than their failures. As students transition to college, these relationships continue to steer them; however, for the first time, they steer students in the wrong directions. The longer that students continue following the comfortable cues that led them to success before college, the more trapped, disoriented, and disgruntled they become in college.

The Three Types of Transition Traps

There are three distinct categories of transition traps. *Structural Traps* encompass the profound influence of the high school classroom. Learning has been defined for them in this environment, and essential lessons about learning have been absorbed through osmosis rather than deliberate intention. As students draw upon these outdated lessons in college, they are misguided and led into clandestine traps. Brace yourself to uncover these hidden lessons and arm yourself with practical strategies to establish the infrastructure students need to achieve maximum academic achievement.

Functional Traps encompass the working relationship students have with their teachers. Armed with expectations for teachers that were forged in the fires of previous educational encounters, students find themselves dazed and confused when these assumptions don't align with how their college teachers function. It is within the realm of functional traps that we shall learn to forge new academic work roles for students, eradicating the pervasive dysfunction that plagues the teacher-student relationship.

Finally, *Cognitive Traps* involve the inadequate mental processes and skills that students attempt to use to do college work. These unwitting learners attempt to conquer the college landscape armed with thinking skills honed in high school, only to discover their incompatibility with the challenges they face. Students soon realize that the skills that got them into college won't sustain them during college. However, they don't know how to access the proper skills. Their frustration festers as their efforts bear little fruit, leaving them either apathetic or indignant. In this section, you will learn how to free students from cognitive traps by empowering them to think strategically and effectively in your course and others.

You should be acutely aware of transition traps because they pose double trouble. These traps undermine not only the students' academic potential but also the very missions and visions of educational institutions. Yet, hope lingers on the horizon, as educators possess the power to liberate students from these confinements. The pages that follow will reveal metacognitive-based approaches, inspirational stories, and transformative solutions to break the chains that bind our students.

As you delve deeper into this invaluable resource, embrace the students' narratives with empathy and glean wisdom from the heroic educators who have liberated their protégés from these snares. Remember, once students break free from these transition traps, their newfound liberation will propel them to extraordinary achievements. Not only will they perform better academically, but they will also rediscover the profound joys of learning, nurturing the seeds of lifelong curiosity and growth.

The journey we embark upon within these pages aims to address the root causes of underperformance, low retention, persistence, and completion rates—those vital metrics by which institutions are judged. Far from a dispassionate clinical view, this book offers an intimate exploration of the very heart of these issues. Each section unveils how a specific trap manifests, empowering teachers to guide their students through the treacherous transition into college.

Become a Choice Architect

Students often find themselves trapped in transition traps due to the contrasting designs of their new college environments compared to their familiar high school settings. As students transition between these two modes of operation, they unwittingly fall prey to the subtle distinctions in design. While it is the students who become entangled in these traps, it is the teachers who unknowingly act as the architects behind them. However, you possess the power to help students navigate past these transition traps by intentionally shaping the architecture of your course.

In their influential work, *Nudge*, behavioral economists Richard Thaler and Cass Sunstein illuminate how the choices and decisions people make are profoundly influenced by the design of their surroundings. According to their perspective, designers establish a default way of operating that individuals automatically accept as the norm. Consequently, designers not only create products or services, but they also wield an immense influence over people's choices, decisions, and lives through the very design of their offerings. Recognizing this tremendous power, Thaler and Sunstein argue that designers bear a responsibility for shaping the context in which individuals make decisions (Thaler & Sunstein, 2009).

The authors illustrate how choice architects have successfully guided people towards better decisions in various domains. For instance, they highlight how a hospital improved employee health by strategically rearranging the order of food items in the cafeteria. By placing healthier options in more accessible locations, they gently nudged individuals towards making healthier choices effortlessly. Similarly, the authors recount how city leaders in Chicago reduced automobile accidents by implementing a simple design intervention. By painting a series of white rumble strips perpendicular to the direction of travel, with each line progressively narrowing as drivers approached the sharpest curve, drivers experienced an illusion of increasing speed. This illusion prompted them to tap their brakes and slow down, thereby reducing accidents along the treacherous curve by an impressive thirty-six percent (Thaler & Sunstein, 2009).

These examples show that the role of a choice architect extends beyond mere functionality. Designers should not only consider how something will function but also contemplate how their design influences people's choices. By deliberately employing design strategies to nudge individuals toward better decisions, you can shape a course environment that empowers students to make optimal choices.

By embracing the principles of choice architecture, you can create an educational experience that guides students away from the perils of transition traps. Just as the placement of healthier food options in a cafeteria can encourage healthier eating habits, your intentional design choices can steer students towards success. With careful consideration and strategic design, you can empower students to navigate the challenges of college with confidence, ensuring their journey is marked by growth, achievement, and fulfillment.

Here's an example of how effective a nudge can be.

Nudging students requires us to hold three points of knowledge in mind simultaneously.

1 We must have an awareness of students' past experiences with academic work.
2 We must be clear about the ideal outcomes we want for students.
3 We must understand the challenge students must overcome to reach the ideal outcomes.

With these three elements in mind, we can create default ways of operating for students that are conducive to our environment. We can be assured that students will use the defaults because they require less decisional cost for students. They choose the best course of action by design.

Throughout this book, I share key features about the ways of thinking and working that have become the default ways of operating for students in high school. I then compare them to new ways of thinking and working that students must employ in college, before sharing ways that we can create new defaults that are compatible with the college environment. I believe that college teachers who have an accurate and empathetic understanding of how students operated in high school are empowered to provide logical solutions, rather than become paralyzed by negative narratives that cast students as lazy or woefully unprepared. As teachers, we must be informed and illuminated by students' past academic experiences. Paul Ramsden, in *Learning to Teach in Higher Education*, admonishes educators, "to become a good teacher, first understand your students' experiences of learning" (Ramsden, 2005). I love his choice of words. He does not advise his colleagues to simply understand the content that students have been exposed to prior to college. No, he encourages them to understand the context in which students have learned the material. I believe that it is impossible to get students to think, learn, and perform their best in college without an accurate understanding of how they did academic work in high school. My more than twenty years of investigating how students do academic work in college has shown me that they are trying to leverage the ways that worked for them in high school during college. They have experienced these methods work for them in the past. But without clarity about the work requirements for the present, they can find themselves struggling due to outdated practices. As teachers, we can nudge them to success by operating as choice architects.

Tools of Choice Architects

As choice architects, our ultimate aim is to guide students towards optimal outcomes without them even realizing they are being nudged. We want the correct choice to be the de facto default choice for students. The key to achieving this goal lies in how we frame the challenges students face. This is where many teachers often misunderstand their role and struggle to effectively help students. While college educators may excel at delivering content, the issue for most students is not learning the content itself. Students have been learning content since their early school years. However, what they haven't learned is how to translate that content into course outcomes. This regulatory process of connecting content, outcomes, and assessments has been traditionally performed for them by their high school teachers. Let me pose a question that I often ask faculty during my workshops.

On a scale of one to five, with one representing "struggles with it all" and five representing "can consistently do it accurately," how well can your students articulate the relationships between your daily instructional content, course outcomes, and course assessments?

If your answer falls above "2" on the scale, I believe your perspective may change as you progress through this book. The most revealing responses come when I ask students and their professors separately. While teachers often rate their students highly in this area, students themselves (once they understand the depth of the question) almost always give themselves lower marks. Many students have never fully grasped these critical relationships, yet they must comprehend them to avoid falling into transition traps.

High school teachers played a crucial role in connecting content, outcomes, and assessments for their students, thus assisting them in regulating their learning. However, college instructors must, at the very least, emphasize the significance of these elements to their students. During my time consulting at Louisiana State University Shreveport in 2015, Dr. Sarah Rahm attended several sessions where I trained learning assistance students to incorporate this regulatory work in their interactions with students. After observing these students in action, Dr. Rahm remarked, "Leonard, attending these sessions has made me realize that faculty are lost. We can't do this for our own courses. How can we expect our students to do it?" She posed a crucial question.

Teachers must forge ahead of their students if they are to help them avoid transition traps. They must make informed decisions when designing their instruction, taking into account students' past and present learning experiences.

I have assisted numerous teachers in applying the principles of choice architecture to their instruction, and I have witnessed the relief they feel when they realize that nudging students yields better learning outcomes than forcefully pushing them. The key design approach for teachers is to adopt a rear-view and windshield perspective when structuring their courses. This entails empathetically considering how students have learned in the past and clearly envisioning the outcomes they need to achieve in the future. With these two perspectives guiding their decisions, teachers can create defaults that strategically nudge students towards making better choices, enhancing their thinking and learning abilities. Teachers who have fully embraced their role as choice architects have observed similar positive outcomes to Thaler and Sunstein, with students making improved decisions effortlessly, without the usual resistance linked to direct appeals for behavioral change.

Operating as choice architects means recognizing that the decisions we make when designing our instruction have a profound impact on the decisions students make when studying and engaging in other academic tasks. It also means taking responsibility for creating the context in which students make their decisions. Lastly, we must establish defaults that serve our students' best interests and are attractive to them, reducing the cognitive burden of decision-making while leading them towards ideal outcomes. In essence, we create nudges. However, effectively nudging students in the present requires us to understand certain aspects of their past experiences and have clarity about what we expect them to accomplish in their future academic work.

TILTing Backward and Forward

It is college teachers' duty to not only understand the content that students have been exposed to prior to college but also the context in which they have learned that material. Recall again Ramsden's emphasis on the importance of fully grasping how students have learned in the past as a predicate to equipping them to learn effectively in the present. This perspective requires us to look beyond a superficial understanding of their previous academic coursework. To truly enable students to think, learn, and perform at their best in college, we must accurately comprehend how they engaged in academic work during their high school years.

One effective framework that college teachers have employed to enhance student learning and performance is the Transparency in Learning and Teaching (TILT) in Higher Education framework introduced by (Winkelmes, 2013). By applying this framework, teachers can significantly improve students' competence, confidence, and performance in assignments. Winkelmes suggests incorporating three additional layers of transparency:

1 Clarifying the purpose of an assignment and explicitly identifying the skills and knowledge that students will acquire through it.
2 Explaining the assignment's objectives and providing clear instructions in plain language.
3 Ensuring that students are aware of the assessment criteria well in advance of the assignment (Angel & Merken, 2021, Winkelmes, 2013).

By implementing these transparency measures, teachers can reduce ambiguity in assignments and grading, dispel misconceptions about required skills, and provide clarity regarding the knowledge students are expected to produce.

While the TILT framework primarily focuses on improving assignment transparency, I believe that students also need transparency about the course as a whole, not just individual assignments. Clearly communicating our expectations is undoubtedly valuable, but it alone is insufficient. It is crucial that we delve into students' past academic experiences.

To illustrate this point, let's consider the example of Chicago's city leaders when developing their nudge for drivers. They had to account for the fact that most drivers attempting the turn believed they were skilled enough to successfully navigate it. Based on their past driving experiences on other roads, they overestimated their ability to make the turn on this specific road. The city leaders had to acknowledge that drivers would overestimate their skills due to their unfamiliarity with the terrain. Traditional solutions like warning signs and flashing lights were ineffective in slowing down drivers. The innovative rumble strips proved to be the perfect nudge.

Similarly, new college students often overestimate their ability to handle college-level work based on their prior academic success. In line with Paul Ramsden's advice, it is crucial for us to understand key aspects of how students have learned in the past. Throughout this book, you will witness the application of Ramsden's wisdom as I incorporate elements of students' past learning experiences into their present college learning process.

Designing Backwards

Expanding on the previous discussions regarding incompatible conditions between high school and college learning environments, as well as the concepts of Nudge and TILT, let's explore the Backward Design Process (BDP) and its significance in instructional design.

Traditionally, teachers followed a linear approach to instruction, where they selected a topic, planned lessons and activities around it, and then

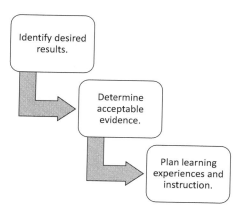

FIGURE 1.1   Stages of the backward design process (Wiggins and McTighe).

created assessments to measure learning outcomes. However, Wiggins and McTighe introduced the Backward Design Process as a transformative alternative (Grant & McTighe, 2001). As the name suggests, BDP reverses the instructional process, starting with the end in mind.

The BDP framework consists of three stages that progressively build upon each other. The first stage involves *identifying the desired results*, which is also referred to as "Beginning with the end in mind." Here, we determine the intended outcomes we want students to achieve by the end of the course. It is essential to focus on the foundational knowledge and abilities that students should demonstrate, rather than solely emphasizing the content to be covered. This stage requires conceptual thinking to develop a clear vision of the course outcomes, which is often overlooked but crucial for effective instruction (Grant & McTighe, 2001).

In the second stage, we move on to *determining acceptable evidence*. This is where we decide on the types of assessments and criteria that align with the desired results established in the first stage. For example, we consider whether students should solve problems, take quizzes, complete comprehensive tests, write papers, or engage in signature assignments. The key is to ensure that the chosen evidence is rooted in the desired results, reinforcing the importance of the work done in the initial stage.

Finally, in the third stage, we *plan learning experiences and instruction*. Here, practical decisions are made regarding the content to be covered, the resources and methods of instruction to be used, and the activities that students will engage in. The organization of materials and instructional strategies should align with the assessments decided upon in stage two, ultimately leading to the achievement of the desired results established in stage one.

The Backward Design Process is fundamentally good design. The reason it is referred to as "backwards" is because it challenges the traditional instructional approach. However, in various aspects of our lives, we naturally engage in backward design. For instance, when building a house, we envision its final appearance before making plans and gathering supplies. Even mundane tasks like selecting an outfit involve a series of thoughts about our desired appearance. Similarly, in teaching, our actions and curriculum should flow from our vision of what we want students to be capable of doing. Understanding that backward design is a common practice in other areas of life can make it easier for us to incorporate the BDP into our instructional design.

By employing the BDP, teachers can avoid common pitfalls such as overwhelming content coverage, textbook-centered teaching, and the use of activities that do not contribute to desired learning outcomes. This approach ensures that instruction is aligned with the intended results and provides clarity, coherence, and purpose throughout the teaching and learning process.

BDP in High School vs BDP in College

The BDP is a widely used instructional model in both high school and college settings. However, key differences between the goals and expectations of high school teachers and college instructors require us to modify the BDP when applied in the college context.

In high school, the primary focus of teachers is to ensure that students are prepared for standardized tests. The success of the school, as well as the teachers themselves, is often tied to how well students perform on these tests. This reality creates a strong incentive for high school teachers to teach to the test, meaning they design their instruction to align closely with the content and format of the assessments. This test-prep approach regulates learning for students, and those who do well in class are likely to perform well on the tests. However, this emphasis on test preparation does not necessarily cultivate independent learners who can think critically and learn on their own, which are essential goals in college.

On the other hand, college instructors have broader goals for their students. They aim to develop critical thinking skills, foster deep learning, promote independent learning, and help students achieve mastery of the

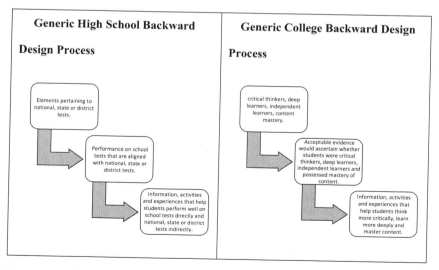

FIGURE 1.2   Generic high school backward design process vs college backward design process.

course content. College teachers focus on creating certain types of learners who can think and learn independently, with minimal assistance. The college environment, with its increased out-of-class time and independence, is designed to support this goal.

Comparison between High School and College Teaching in Stage 1 of the BDP

The difference in goals between high school and college has significant implications for the application of the BDP. In high school, the first stage of the BDP, which involves identifying desired results, is strongly driven by the need to prepare students for tests. High school teachers invest significant class time in activities and lessons that directly align with the test content, ensuring that students are test-ready. In this context, teaching to the test makes sense given the incentives and constraints that high school teachers face.

Jal Mehta and Sarah Fine (2019) conducted a six-year study of a diverse range of high schools across the country. These schools were known for producing students who excelled on high-stakes exams. Initially, Mehta and Fine intended to uncover the practices that contributed to these students' deep thinking and learning abilities. However, upon visiting these highly acclaimed schools, they were surprised to find a lack of substantial deep thinking and learning. This realization led them to rename their book to *In Search of Deeper Learning*. Throughout their investigation, Mehta and Fine observed that the mental labor undertaken by students in these renowned schools did not align with the type of mental labor required in college. Although students were well-prepared to pass tests, they lacked the skills to learn independently, which is a crucial objective in college.

In college, the first stage of the BDP takes on a different meaning. College instructors focus on defining the desired outcomes in terms of critical thinking, deep learning, and independent learning. The emphasis shifts from test preparation to fostering the skills and abilities that will enable students to become self-directed learners. College teachers expect students to take more responsibility for their own learning and prepare themselves for assessments. As a college teacher, perhaps you've experienced the effects of the high school backwards design process in two specific ways: (1) when students ask that most despised question, "Is this going to be on the test," and (2) when students waste their time in between classes and then complain that they don't have enough time to study. Students are acting on the default learning metrics that have guided them throughout their educational experience thus far. Since tests in their past have primarily assessed them on the inputs that were presented during class, they believe that college will be the same. Of course, they expect to be required to learn more inputs, but they don't expect that they will have to do something qualitatively different, such as produce new outcomes with the inputs. Yet, they must make this shift quickly upon entering college. Making this shift requires that they make new relationships with the environment, with their teachers and with academic work. Failure to make this shift will leave them trapped.

Comparison between High School and College Teaching in Stage 2 of the BDP

The second stage of the BDP, determining acceptable evidence, also differs between high school and college. In high school, evidence often comes in the form of tests that directly assess the content taught in class. Students are accustomed to relying on their teachers for test preparation, and the activities and interactions in high school are designed to meet this goal. In college, the goal is to develop critical thinking and mastery of content, so the types of evidence required may vary. This is the reason that the tests that students encounter in college are fundamentally different from those in high school. Since college teachers are not playing the test-prep role, students must use qualitatively different types of mental labor and insights.

Comparison between High School and College Teaching in Stage 3 of the BDP

The third stage of the BDP, planning learning experiences and instruction, may superficially resemble high school instruction in terms of lectures, information-rich slides, and problem sets. However, these activities serve different purposes in college. Students need to engage in a different type of mental labor to extract the insights and outcomes that college instructors are seeking. The structural and infrastructural differences between high school and college instruction are deeply embedded, and students may not initially recognize the shift in expectations.

Understanding these differences between high school and college instruction is crucial for college teachers to effectively help students transition and succeed. By recognizing the gaps and traps that students may encounter, instructors can design their instruction in a way that supports the development of independent learners who can thrive in the college learning environment. Adjusting the BDP to align with the unique goals and expectations of college education can contribute to a smoother transition and better outcomes for students.

The Basis of This Book

The premise of this book is that colleges and universities can effectively address academic performance and retention issues by preventing students from falling into transition traps. Before delving into the insights presented in this book, I, like many others in the field of education, felt helpless in supporting students. This sentiment was echoed at conferences and workshops nationwide, where numerous college educators shared their similar experiences. Regardless of location, I encountered groups of teachers who believed that solving this problem was beyond their control, adopting what I refer to as the "Papa Johns" method of instruction "Give me better students, and I'll deliver better results." These educators had tried various instructional improvements over the years, but none had substantially enhanced student performance. Consequently, they had resigned themselves to the notion that students were simply ill-equipped for college-level work, and, to some extent, they were correct. Acknowledging that a force hinders students from achieving the success they strive for is crucial. We all have our theories about why certain students excel in college while others struggle. Some ideas are based on research, while others stem from personal observations and experiences. Most of our notions are a blend of our experiences, aligned with our beliefs and supported by research. Unfortunately, we often prioritize one explanation over others. For instance, when *The Shallows: What the Internet is Doing to Our Brains* was published in 2011, many campuses fixated on the idea that students' academic difficulties were a result of their supposedly compromised ability to concentrate. Then, following the release of "GRIT: The Power of Passion and Perseverance" in 2016, the higher education community became enamored with fostering students' resilience and determination. Now, in the aftermath of the COVID-19 pandemic, the challenge lies in helping students overcome presumed significant gaps in their knowledge. I understand why perspectives like these resonate with college educators, as they provide an external factor to blame for students' struggles, absolving and validating us in the process. Over the years, I have worked with numerous schools facing a state of paralysis due to negative narratives. Widespread academic underperformance led them to conclude that their students were incapable of learning. However, during the course of our consultations, their perspective gradually shifted. They began to see their students in a new light, developing greater empathy and a sense of empowerment. I believe this transformation occurs as they start viewing the academic environment through the lenses of my research, which I refer to as my research cocktail.

My Research Cocktail

In the medical field, certain diseases prove to be exceptionally resistant and cannot be effectively treated with a single drug. To combat such stubborn ailments, doctors often rely on a medical cocktail—a carefully orchestrated combination of drugs administered in a specific sequence. This strategic approach unleashes a force multiplier effect, eradicating the disease and restoring the patient's health. Inspired by this concept, I have crafted a research cocktail—a unique blend of research constructs—that empowers educators and students to gain enhanced clarity on the intricate mental mechanisms underlying academic work, particularly in navigating the challenges of transition traps.

Similar to the sequential administration of drugs in a medical cocktail, the research doses presented in this cocktail are designed to be utilized in a specific order, synergistically augmenting each other's effects. By sequentially integrating these research constructs, educators can unlock valuable insights into the academic experiences of their students and foster an environment that facilitates growth and success.

My research cocktail, which consists of five key research constructs that are interwoven throughout this book, help me clearly understand the intricate mental mechanisms underlying academic work, and they have provided other educators clarity about what is happening in their environments as well. When I consult with institutions, the faculty, staff, administrators, and students often express that one of the most valuable contributions I make is providing them with a language to discuss their experiences more precisely. However, I believe that my true impact lies in offering them a sharper lens through which to view their experiences, and their newfound language serves as validation that they are indeed seeing their environment through new perspectives.

As I share my research cocktail with you, be mindful that these constructs are deeply embedded in the issues that affect student learning and performance, appearing in every section of this book. Like main characters in a play who reappear in different ways throughout the performance, these constructs manifest differently but consistently throughout the book.

Approaches to Learning

Have you ever felt like you and your students were always on different pages? Like trying to play music together but reading from different sheets? Have you and your colleagues struggled to understand why a student excels in one teacher's course but struggles in another's? Perhaps you attributed their success to greater interest or background knowledge in certain subjects, or even labeled one teacher's course as "easy." What you may not have realized is that you and your students have unknowingly been entangled in a crucial research construct known as approaches to learning.

This construct is widely researched and practiced in many countries where high school students consistently outperform those in the United States, such as Australia, Canada, China, Korea, Finland, and New Zealand (PISA, 2018). However, in my experience, I find that only a relative few researchers or educators in the United States truly understand this construct. As teachers, we must familiarize ourselves with approaches to learning because it plays a fundamental role in every aspect of the teaching and learning dynamic.

So, what exactly is an approach to learning? Let me break it down to explain why it is a central element of my research cocktail. An approach is a viewpoint or perspective on what something is and how it works. We can have an approach about anything. For example, in relationships, one person may have a direct approach, tackling dilemmas head-on, while another person may have an indirect approach, preferring to beat around the bush. In business, one company may adopt a laissez-faire approach, resulting in lenient policies, while another may take an interventionist approach, implementing proactive measures. The approach or viewpoint governs all actions, so understanding it is crucial if we want to comprehend why individuals operating within a particular approach behave the way they do.

The approach is of paramount importance as it establishes an organization's culture. In academic environments, an institution's approach shapes the culture inside and outside the classroom. But what happens when students have a different academic culture than we do? What if their perspectives are incompatible with ours? These fundamental differences create a perpetual clash of cultures. I used to wonder why students seemed to interpret class material differently from me. However, once I understood that their approach to academic work differed from mine, these clashes started making sense. And when I shared this knowledge with students, lectures transformed into deep dialogs, and they became less concerned with passing tests and more focused on genuine learning.

Two Types of Approaches to Learning

An approach to learning represents a fundamental view of what learning is, how it operates, and what is required to learn. Our approach stems from core epistemological and philosophical assumptions about the nature of learning, the purpose of education, and how knowledgeable individuals function. Researchers have categorized approaches to learning into two types: surface and deep.

A surface approach is based on the belief that learning consists primarily of accumulating facts. Under a surface approach, contextual understanding and other mental processes necessary for comprehension are often absent (Biggs, 1987, Eklund-Myrkog, 1997, Tait, 2009). On the other hand, a deep approach reflects an intention to connect learning in more meaningful ways and to develop a holistic understanding. When operating from a deep approach, individuals seek to discern relationships among different pieces of information.

When my students were trapped within a surface approach, their primary concern was copying and memorizing notes. From their perspective, learning meant holding information in their mental warehouse until I assessed them, and they expected the assessment to focus solely on what we covered in class. However, my approach involved assessing them on a broader range of material, as the class content served as a foundation rather than an exhaustive list. When I shared this perspective with them, they were completely perplexed, and rightfully so, because their understanding aligned with how school typically functions when viewed through a surface approach.

With a firm grasp of approaches to learning, I began to understand the recurring conflicts that permeate the relationships between college teachers and students. Most college teachers operate from a deep approach to learning, expecting and rewarding meaningful interactions. This may manifest as engaging class discussions that delve into multiple concepts, with the outcome often remaining undetermined at the end of a class session. Students operating from a surface approach, however, may find such expectations bewildering. This is evident when students inquire if the material covered will be included in the test—a question that tends to frustrate us. Yet, it often signifies the prevalence of surface approaches among our students. In the section on Functional Traps, you will discover how students' surface approaches establish intricate networks of schemas and scripts that clash with our deep approach, making harmonious learning nearly impossible. It's important to remember that our students are not inherently deficient or incapable—they are simply viewing the academic environment through the lens of their surface approach, which has been their primary learning perspective.

Throughout this book, you will witness the conflicts that arise when approaches to learning are misaligned between teachers and students. However, you will also witness the transformative power of learning when students shift to a deep approach. In this state, they embrace complex work and deploy the necessary skills to excel. As professors shared in my one-month check-in session, when students transitioned to a deep approach, their focus shifted from simply earning a grade to assessing their own learning. They willingly put in more effort, becoming eager to face greater academic challenges. (You can watch college professors discuss this experience in my

Metacognitive Teaching Tactics 1-Month Check-in video on my YouTube channel) (Geddes, 2022).

Mental Representation

Have you ever pondered how students can get information so wrong on assessments that you painstakingly covered during class? These experiences leave us thinking, "what is going on in their heads?" "Did they pay attention at all in class?" When what students know differs from what you presented, then they likely are suffering from faulty mental representations. *Mental representations* refer to the informational impressions that remain after students have interacted with new information (Pitt, 2019). These representations serve as the mind's interpretation or imitation of the information or experiences encountered.

Aristotle first recognized the power of mental representation in his work *De Anima* where he says, "thinking is different from perceiving and is held to be, in part, imagination" (Aristotle, 1984). Mental representations link our thinking and imagination, a critical union in academic work. However, mental representations are not actively engaged during the actual experience; instead, they become active when we use our imaginative functions to anticipate future events or recall past ones. They play a crucial role in academic work, connecting our thinking and imagination. However, students often focus more on accumulating notes during class rather than actively assessing the accuracy of their mental representations of the content. This can hinder their learning process, regardless of their intelligence or dedication.

It is important to consider students' awareness of their mental representations before and after class. Before class, students may have preconceived notions or existing mental representations of the content to be covered. During class, these representations take a backseat as other cognitive processes, such as concentration and engagement, take precedence. After class, students rely on their mental representations when studying and engaging in subsequent academic work. This distinction between what is covered in class and how it is represented in students' minds is crucial in understanding why their knowledge often deviates from what was taught.

In my experience, students often start with inaccurate mental representations due to their surface approach to learning. Their shallow representations align with their surface learning style, which prioritizes superficial knowledge over deep understanding. When they study afterward, instead of deepening their knowledge, they simply reinforce the shallow knowledge they have already produced, creating a feedback loop that perpetuates their underperformance.

Previously, I used to wonder what happened to the information covered in class when students were away from the classroom. In class, things seemed to "click." Many times, I felt like they understood the content relatively well. They did too! And then their performance on assessments would disappoint both of us. I now realize that students were often developing poorly constructed mental representations of the material, which hinders their ability to apply knowledge accurately. To address this issue, I developed a 360-degree approach that enhances students' mental representation skills.

By implementing precoding and consolidation techniques, I was able to improve students' mental representations of the course content. This subtle tweak had a significant impact on their learning outcomes. For instance, Suzanna James, a sophomore nursing student, was initially struggling academically and was on the verge of being asked to leave the program. However, after implementing the new techniques, Suzanna experienced a positive transformation. She expressed feeling more capable of comprehending and learning all of the courses outcomes, despite being at the beginning of the semester. Her test scores also demonstrated the impact of improved mental representations:

Exam #1: 73
Intervention Session
Exam #2: 96
Exam #3: 94
Exam #4: 99

Mental representation, combined with approaches to learning, reveals the structural and functional traps that hinder students who rely solely on their high school perspectives and perception skills. Students often lack the necessary cognitive infrastructure to produce high-quality mental representations. This gap becomes a challenging transition for students.

Mental representation serves as a critical metric for education. Once the study session is over or the educational process is complete, all students have left is their mind's capacity to mentally represent what they have learned and use these representations for studying and preparation. If their mental representations are incorrect or faulty, it becomes challenging for them to learn the material correctly.

Now, we move on to the most significant component of the research cocktail: metacognition. This construct highlights the ongoing challenge students face in aligning their thinking with the depth of thinking required for academic tasks.

Metacognition

The most consequential dosage of the cocktail is *metacognition*. This construct sheds light on the perpetual challenge students face in aligning their thinking with the required thinking for academic tasks.

Metacognition refers to the awareness and understanding of one's own thought processes. It is often described as "thinking about thinking," and has its roots in the seminal work of John Flavell (Flavell, 1976). While metacognition is one of the most well-researched academic work constructs, many educators have only a superficial understanding of it. This shallow understanding leads them to attempt to cover for learning and performance deficiencies by layering thinking words in their syllabi or including thinking skills verbiage in instruction. A comprehensive understanding of metacognition involves learners' knowledge and awareness of their internal processes, states, and conditions as they engage with information and navigate tasks within their learning environments (Hennessey, 1999, Kuhn, 2004, Martinez, 2006). Furthermore, metacognition involves reflecting on and monitoring one's thinking, as well as making adjustments and employing strategies to enhance learning and problem-solving (Flavell, 1979).

This broader view of metacognition synthesizes the personal awareness, task awareness, and regulatory components of metacognitive processes. It goes beyond cognitive work and delves into the deeper aspects of students' cognition, which ultimately requires students to connect their internal experiences with the external demands of their learning. Metacognition is the mental mechanism that enables students to gain control over these relationships, ultimately leading to superb learning outcomes.

Metacognition is the bridge that connects approaches to learning and mental representations, allowing students to navigate their cognitive processes effectively. When students possess metacognitive skills, they are able to assess their understanding of the material, identify knowledge gaps, and deploy appropriate strategies to bridge those gaps. However, many students lack metacognitive awareness, which hinders their ability to accurately gauge their own learning. This is especially true for surface learners who focus on memorization and reproduction of information, rather than deeper comprehension.

Metacognition plays a crucial role in the formation and refinement of mental representations. Without metacognitive monitoring, students may have faulty or shallow mental representations of the material they have encountered. They might believe they understand a concept when, in reality, their understanding is superficial. This misalignment between perceived comprehension and actual comprehension can lead to poor performance on assessments and a failure to transfer knowledge to new contexts.

Metacognition surpasses other constructs by not only enhancing student engagement but also fundamentally transforming how students interact with information, resulting in definitive improvements in learning outcomes and performance. In a study conducted by Hall and Webster (2008), it was demonstrated that an increase in students' metacognitive skills leads to enhanced self-efficacy. This indicates that when we cultivate students' metacognitive skills, they not only achieve better results but also develop a greater sense of competence and confidence in their academic abilities. Young and Fry (2008) succinctly capture the role of metacognition in helping students avoid engaging in pseudowork, which refers to tasks that do not produce meaningful learning outcomes. Metacognition is the agent that transforms the actions of studiousness—attending class, reading material, studying, taking notes and the like—into systematically measurable and definable learning outcomes (Young & Fry, 2008). The prevalence of pseudowork among college students is further discussed in the Pseudowork chapter. Reflecting on her experience, Kristina, a student at Denison University, summarized the impact of metacognition by stating, "It never occurred to me that the way I was thinking and processing information may not align with my professors' expectations, and thus could be making a course more difficult for me than it needs to be." Once Kristina gained control over her metacognitive processes, her mental representations about the course material were clearer and deeper. Consequently, she was able to study more efficiently, resulting in improved learning and performance.

In summary, metacognition has been found to correlate positively with academic achievement across various educational contexts and age groups (Efklides, 2011, Moseley et al., 2005). Students who engage in metacognitive practices demonstrate deeper comprehension, critical thinking skills, and the ability to transfer knowledge to new situations (Baker, 2009, Flavell, 1979, Nelson, 1990).

You will notice metacognition's fingerprints throughout this book. In the Cognitive Traps section, you will see examples of how teachers have leveraged metacognitive practices to significantly improve student performance. Also, you will see how shifting to a deep approach to learning and using higher order thinking skills work in tandem to enhance students' mental representation skills, and you will see how metacognition ultimately helps students engage in effective learning transfer, which is the next construct in my research cocktail.

Transfer of Learning

The fourth dose in my research cocktail focuses on the concept of *transfer of learning*. This construct is essential for understanding the external outcomes of academic work and how students apply what they have learned in one context to another (Snowman, 2006). Transfer of learning is at the core of the learning process because we acquire knowledge with the intention of using it in future situations.

To illustrate this, let's consider Margie, a five-year-old who has just learned to play a musical note on an instrument. When Margie attempts to play the same note again in a different situation or context, she engages in transfer. If she successfully replicates the skill, it demonstrates positive transfer. However, if she is unable to play the note, it indicates negative transfer (Perkins, 1992, Snowman, 2006).

Understanding transfer of learning helps us comprehend why certain aspects of students' learning manifest properly on assessments while others do not. In essence, our assessments aim to measure how effectively students engage in positive transfer. Researchers have categorized two types of transfer: *near transfer* and *far transfer* (Snowman, 2006). Near transfer occurs when we apply knowledge or skills learned in one context to a similar context, while far transfer involves applying knowledge to a significantly different context.

It's important to recognize that the context plays a crucial role in determining the success of transfer. As the context changes between the antecedent and subsequent episodes, the transfer experience can shift from near to far transfer. The greater the change between contexts, the more challenging the transfer becomes.

Near transfer experiences are more likely to result in positive transfer because they involve relatively similar contexts, allowing students to apply their learning more consistently. On the other hand, far transfer experiences are more likely to result in negative transfer because they involve significantly different contexts, making success less probable. Many students underperform because they are unknowingly stuck in far transfer traps, as you will discover in the *Far Transfer Traps* chapter.

Let's revisit Margie's experience to explore how changes in context shift her from positive near transfer to negative far transfer. If Margie attempts to play the note a few minutes after learning it, it represents a near transfer experience, and she is likely to succeed. The factors contributing to near transfer in this scenario are the replication of a recently learned skill and the involvement of short-term memory, which are both relatively low-level cognitive skills.

However, if we change the factors, such as increasing the time between the antecedent and subsequent episode to 24 hours, Margie can no longer rely solely on her short-term memory. This change in context requires her to employ additional strategies to increase the chances of positive transfer.

Similarly, if we ask Margie to play the note on a different instrument while keeping the time the same, such as handing her a saxophone instead of the instrument she learned on, she may struggle to complete the task. Students often feel the same way when confronted with far transfer situations. Surprisingly, practically every assessment we give students can be considered a far transfer experience, as you will discover throughout this book, because the outcomes we assess are qualitatively different from the inputs we provide.

While many educators think about transfer of learning from a programmatic or institutional perspective, encompassing how students' performance in one course translates to another or how their school knowledge applies to the workplace, these views are not exhaustive (Snowman, 2006). Transfer of learning is a fundamental process of applying what we have learned from one context to another.

In this book, we will examine transfer of learning using three different contexts: in-class exposure, academic work, and assessment. By recognizing how changes in context can set students up for far transfer traps, we can help them convert these challenges into near transfer experiences. The aim is to assist students in connecting their learning experiences across various contexts and ensuring their knowledge comes full circle.

As we delve further into the book, you will witness the effects of transfer of learning manifesting. There is also a dedicated chapter that outlines how students become trapped in transfer of learning traps, offering strategies to help them navigate these challenges.

Recall that our research cocktail began with approaches to learning, understanding how students interpret academic experiences differently. Then, we explored how students' mental representation of content influences their outcomes. Metacognition allowed us to address students' internal processing and connect it with external task demands. Now, transfer of learning completes the picture, empowering students to take ownership of their academic work and responsibility for their learning. To fully grasp this effect, we must consider the concept of locus of control. Therefore, in our final dose, we will explore locus of control and its impact on student engagement and motivation.

Locus of Control

In 2014, I had the opportunity to work closely with a group of high school students at Hickory High School, located in western North Carolina. During a thought-provoking focus group session, I sought to understand why these students believed they performed poorly in a specific class. Their immediate response was that they had "a bad teacher." At first glance, it seemed like a suitable self-serving reaction, suggesting that the students were unwilling to take responsibility for their own failures. However, my perspective underwent a significant shift when I asked them to explain the reasons behind their success in other classes. To my surprise, they attributed their achievements to having "a good teacher." It became apparent that these students were not merely evading accountability or denying credit for their successes. Instead, they genuinely felt that they had minimal control over their academic performance.

This realization was not unique to high school students alone. Through my consulting work, I discovered that college students often share similar sentiments. They perceive themselves as lacking control over their academic outcomes, instead attributing that control to their teachers or external factors. This overwhelming feeling of powerlessness contributes to the prevalent apathy and disengagement we often encounter among our students.

Have you ever wondered why students feel powerless to control their performance? Understanding the concept of *locus of control* offers valuable insights into why students feel so disempowered in their academic pursuits. Coined by Julian B. Rotter in 1966, locus of control examines the extent to which individuals believe their actions influence the outcomes of various situations (Rotter, 1966). Those who possess an internal locus of control firmly believe in their ability to shape future outcomes and tend to exhibit high internal motivation for achievement. Conversely, individuals with an external locus of control perceive outcomes as being beyond their control, often spending considerable time trying to explain their failures (Zaidi & Moshin, 2013).

As educators, it is crucial to recognize that many of our college students arrive on campus with an external locus of control. A telltale sign of this undesirable condition is their tendency to blame others, including their teachers, for their struggles. When students point fingers at us as the cause of their academic challenges, it is an indication that they feel powerless and trapped within an external locus of control. However, there is no need for concern. The metacognitive-based strategies presented in this book can provide us with the tools to empower students to take ownership of their academic work.

Before we can effectively assist our students, it is vital that we, as educators, engage in a self-assessment and avoid succumbing to an external locus of control ourselves. The feeling of powerlessness is not a conducive space for us to occupy. If both we and our students feel powerless, who will take charge of establishing the proper teaching and learning dynamics? Without a sense of agency in academic environments, the learning experience is likely to drift aimlessly. A firsthand encounter with the consequences of an external locus of control came through my interaction with Dr. John Sage, a brilliant young professor who found himself in an unfortunate situation.

Dr. Sage had recently received prestigious recognition for his teaching in May. Administrators read glowing reviews from students, highlighting how Dr. Sage's class had positively impacted their learning. However, when September arrived, marking the start of a new academic year, Dr. Sage's class took an unexpected turn. He confided in me, expressing his deep dissatisfaction with one particular class. When I inquired about his plans to alter the dynamics of the class, he admitted to having tried everything within his repertoire, yet the situation remained unfavorable. He even lamented that both he and his students had resigned themselves to accepting that the class would suck. It was disheartening to witness a talented teacher like Dr. Sage embracing such a negative circumstance so early in the semester. No teacher should ever have to endure a sucky class, as we possess the power to effect change and transform the trajectory of our classrooms.

While your own experiences may not mirror the extreme circumstances faced by Dr. Sage, it is essential to recognize that any perception of power-lessness reflects an external locus of control. When we find ourselves complaining about our students without acknowledging the significant impact we have on the learning environment, we unintentionally abdicate our agency. Our intentions are not to neglect our power; rather, we often fail to perceive it. As you progress through this book, my hope is that you will no longer view your students as deficient or incapable. Instead, focus on leveraging their existing knowledge and skills. Most importantly, rediscover your own power as an educator—a bridge capable of guiding students away from the transition traps they may encounter. When you witness students caught between the successes of their past and the promises of their future, you have the opportunity to be the bridge that helps them reach their fullest academic potential.

SECTION I

Structural Traps

During a flight to a National Science Foundation (NSF) conference at Northwestern University in May 2017, I found myself seated next to Vickie, a mother whose son was entering his senior year of high school. As Vickie glanced over at my computer screen, she caught a glimpse of a few slides from my presentation on college student performance. Intrigued by the information, she struck up a conversation with me about my line of work. When I mentioned that I was a consultant specializing in helping good high school students succeed in college, Vickie gave me a perplexed look. It was a look I had grown accustomed to receiving from both educators and workshop participants. However, Vickie was the first to verbalize her curiosity, asking, "Why would a successful high school student struggle in college?"

Her question struck a chord with me, as it aligned perfectly with the central question driving my research over the past two decades. Eager to delve into the topic, I explained to Vickie that the way learning takes place in high school often clashes with the demands of the college environment. Consequently, many students who excelled in high school encounter difficulties when it comes to learning in college. Recognizing the constraints of our short flight, I chose to simplify the explanation by likening the high school learning experience to a conveyer belt. In high school, teachers are expected to go above and beyond to facilitate student learning and success, creating an environment where students can operate on autopilot. Naturally, students carry this expectation with them to college. However, college professors have a different perspective. They believe that it is the students' responsibility to navigate their own path to learning and success.

DOI: 10.4324/9781003447252-2

As Vickie contemplated this comparison, she shared some insights about her son, Kareem, who was soon to graduate from high school. She described him as a studious young man, consistently earning top grades in advanced classes throughout his K–12 years with an impressive GPA of over 4.2. So far, everything seemed promising for Kareem. Vickie proudly mentioned that he rarely had to do schoolwork at home due to his natural abilities.

At that moment, a hint of concern arose within me regarding Kareem's future in college. After engaging in some friendly mom-bragging, Vickie finally asked me the question she had been leading up to: Did I think Kareem would be okay in college? Wanting to alleviate her worries, I reassured her with a smile, expressing confidence in Kareem's preparedness. Vickie closed her eyes, taking a moment to rest.

However, I must admit that I wasn't entirely truthful with Vickie that day. Deep down, I had doubts about Kareem's smooth transition into college. My skepticism didn't stem from a pessimistic view of students, but rather from the structural challenges that many high-achieving high school students encounter when navigating the college landscape. As they leave the familiar structure and comforting infrastructure elements that facilitated academic work in high school, they encounter a work structure and environment that is different and difficult to navigate. Unable to properly discern the differences, they become trapped, frozen between the student they were and the learner they must become.

Structural Traps Introduction

The structure and infrastructure of organizations significantly shape the nature of work and directly impact employees' ability to perform high-quality work. In an organizational context, structure refers to the arrangement of working relationships and the division of responsibilities. While these elements are often invisible and overlooked, they provide the framework for how people will collaborate and complete tasks. On the other hand, infrastructure encompasses the physical and technological resources, tools, and systems that support the employees' work processes. The infrastructure serves as the backbone of the work. It helps the organization run smoothly and enables employees to get work done more efficiently.

Similarly, within the academic realm, the structure and infrastructure of a classroom play a vital role in students' ability to produce quality work. A well-designed structure provides a clear framework for the work tasks and relational expectations, while the infrastructure includes elements like the syllabus, instructional materials, and learning resources that support the learning process. Just as an organized and well-equipped organization enhances productivity and success, a classroom's structure and infrastructure are essential for enabling students to work productively, engage with the subject matter effectively, and achieve academic success.

During the transition from high school to college, students often face various challenges that hinder their success in the new academic environment. One common challenge they encounter is the presence of Structural Traps. These traps arise when the structure and infrastructure of the college classroom do not align with the demands of academic work. These invisible barriers can sabotage students' work from the start and impede their academic success.

If we want more college students to thrive, then it is crucial to provide a work structure and infrastructure that effectively support the type of knowledge construction required at the college level. When the structure is unclear or when needed elements are missing, it is nearly impossible for students to discern the work requirements. Additionally, when the infrastructure system is inadequate, solvable problems can pester students and teachers, causing even capable students to needlessly struggle.

As students navigate this transition, they must adapt their previous academic approaches to the new demands they face. This phase becomes a critical juncture, with many students finding themselves trapped and rapidly descending into a spiral of academic challenges.

How Structural Traps Affect Students

The academic achievements of students like Kareem demonstrate their ability to succeed in the high school environment. However, when transitioning to college, students may encounter challenges due to differences in classroom structures and inadequate adjustments by their college teachers. These structural traps can have a significant impact on students' performance, impeding their progress and hindering their ability to learn effectively.

One crucial aspect affected by structural traps is the lack of clarity in students' learning targets. Without a suitable class structure and complementary infrastructure elements, students struggle to define clear objectives for their academic work. As a result, they may feel disconnected between in-class and out-of-class activities, leading to disengagement and a sense of frustration.

Role confusion is another consequence of structural traps. Students may find it challenging to understand the specific work and responsibilities expected of them within the course. This lack of clarity can further hinder their ability to effectively navigate the learning process and meet the course requirements.

Furthermore, when the structure is misaligned and infrastructure elements are absent, students may experience outcome confusion. This occurs when they mistake leverage points for the learning outcomes of their course.

Confusion regarding what truly constitutes a successful outcome can lead to misguided efforts and potentially unsatisfactory learning experiences.

In summary, structural traps significantly impact students' academic journey by impeding clarity, fostering role confusion, and inducing outcome confusion. It is crucial for educators and institutions to recognize and address these traps to ensure that students have a clear path to their learning destinations and can thrive in their academic pursuits.

How Structural Traps Affect Teachers

Structural traps have a detrimental impact on educators as well. In my experience consulting with various schools, I have observed faculty expressing dissatisfaction with the ineffectiveness of previous professional development initiatives. Let me share an example from 2016 when I submitted a proposal to a large state university aiming to improve its historically low graduation rate of around 28 percent. Despite advising them on the stifling effect of structural traps on student performance and faculty frustration, the provost decided to invest nearly one and a half million dollars in implementing a popular program. Fast forward five years, during the SACSCOC Annual Meeting where I was the keynote speaker, a faculty member from that institution informed me about the consequences of ignoring my advice. He revealed that not only did it cost the institution a substantial amount of money, but it also significantly impacted morale. The graduation rate remained stagnant, and the pressure among faculty reached an all-time high.

When structural traps persist, it places an excessive workload on faculty. Without a proper structure and supporting infrastructure, teachers are forced to overcompensate by investing a considerable amount of effort into reteaching concepts either during class or during office hours. This increased workload coupled with a high-stress, low-reward environment often leads to conflicts among faculty members. Allow me to illustrate this with an example from 2011, when tensions between faculty and athletic coaches had escalated to the point where the provost sought my assistance in resolving the issue. After engaging with students, faculty, and coaches, it became evident that structural traps were insidiously driving a wedge between them. However, by promptly implementing a program that identified and eliminated these traps, the institution experienced remarkable changes. From 2012 to 2020, the institution led its conference in student-athlete performance, including football and men's basketball, which had previously struggled with low GPAs more than any other athletic team. Most notably, by 2014, just three years later, faculty were conducting workshops on the rewards of working with student-athletes. This success story highlights the pernicious nature of structural traps: they turn potential allies into adversaries. However, when we address and remove these traps from the educational environment, teachers can rediscover the joys of teaching, and students can reap the rewards of meaningful learning experiences.

Finally, structural traps have a profound impact on both students and teachers, creating significant challenges within the classroom environment. Students find themselves struggling to navigate unclear expectations and disconnected learning experiences, leading to disengagement and confusion. Meanwhile, teachers bear the burden of overcompensating for inadequate structures, resulting in increased workload and strained relationships. The insidious nature of structural traps can turn allies into adversaries, hindering student success and diminishing the joy of teaching. To foster a conducive learning environment, it is imperative to identify and eliminate these traps, allowing students to thrive and teachers to fully embrace their role as facilitators of knowledge. By removing these barriers, we can create a classroom where learning flourishes, collaboration thrives, and both students and teachers can experience the true rewards of education.

This section sheds light on the structural disparities between high school and college, highlighting the early obstacles that hinder students' success. To begin, I provide a concise definition of academic work, and distill it into a fundamental, universally applicable formula that works for any academic course students will take. Next, I share the critical roles that structure and infrastructure play in academic work, emphasizing their impact on student learning and performance. Then, I use the High School vs. College Environment Comparison Chart to illustrate the differences between how work gets done between the two environments, showcasing how the Academic Work Formula applies distinctively to each environment. This introductory overview will prepare you for the subsequent chapters in this section.

The first chapter, titled "Workspace Traps," delves into the role of the workspace component in facilitating students' learning and performance in high school classrooms. We will then explore the challenges that arise from the absence of structural necessity in college classrooms. Next, I share practical strategies for how you can establish new workspaces that foster an environment suitable for college-level academic work. By addressing the structural barriers that impede student success, you will create engaging and productive learning environments that propel students to do high-quality academic work.

In the subsequent chapter, we explore the Division of Labor traps. These ruses manifest in students' beliefs that the responsibility for learning is solely on the teacher, leading to a passive and dependent approach to academic work. Students trapped in Division of Labor traps often expect the teacher to provide step-by-step instructions, study guides, and all the answers, while neglecting their own role in the learning process. These traps hinder students' development of critical thinking, problem-solving skills, and independent learning capabilities. I share a choice architecture approach you can use to ensuring students are laboring properly when engaged in academic work. By understanding and addressing the Division of Labor traps, you can empower students to take ownership of their learning journey and foster a more active and engaged learning environment.

In the concluding chapter of this section, we delve into the Locus of Learning Trap, which centers on students' beliefs regarding the responsibility for their own learning. We address the scheduling delusion that hinders students and takes away precious time. This chapter culminates with the "Managing the Daylight Hours" schedule, which is designed to help students develop a crucial skill needed for college academic work: managing their time effectively during daylight hours. You can use this schedule to help students create a balance between their academic commitments and recreational activities, allowing them to find both productivity and enjoyment in their busy academic lives.

By recognizing and addressing different structural traps presented in this section, you can help students take ownership of their learning and cultivate a sense of agency in their academic journey.

What Is Academic Work?

If you search for what academic work entails, you will likely find several esoteric definitions that start like this, "Academic work involves both the pursuit of knowledge and its dissemination and application through activities … (Council, 2022)." While definitions such as these may be technically accurate, they don't capture the essence of the type of work that college students and teachers do together. In my perspective, academic work can be categorized as *knowledge work*, where knowledge serves as the main input into the work, the primary means of achieving the work, and the major output of the work (Newell, Robertson, Scarbrough, & Swan, 2002). This broader definition aligns well with the activities that take place in educational settings. Teachers provide students with inputs in the form of content, and students utilize their mental resources, such as knowledge-making skills, to process these inputs. Ultimately, students produce outcomes in the form of knowledge products, which serve as evidence of their acquired knowledge. To condense this definition, I have formulated it as follows:

Academic Work Formula

Inputs + Processing = Outcomes

FIGURE S1.1   Academic Work Formula

Academic work presents challenges because all aspects—inputs, processing, and outcomes—are intricately connected and involve knowledge. It is comparable to pouring water into a glass while submerged underwater; separating one aspect of the work from another is difficult. Moreover, what makes academic work even more complex is the interdependence between teachers and students; they must achieve mental alignment on each of the formula's elements to collaboratively create the work products.

High school graduates often struggle to adapt to academic work in college due to the changes in the formula within the college environment. College introduces students to a greater quantity and variety of inputs. Additionally, students must employ a more sophisticated set of thinking skills to process these inputs. Furthermore, the outcomes expected from students in college tend to be qualitatively deeper than those in high school. Throughout this book, you will discover the broad applicability of the academic work formula. At this stage, it is crucial to understand that the structural and infrastructural changes in academic work during the college years require students to employ the formula differently than they did in high school. As teachers, we can support students by making them aware of these changes and assisting them in navigating this new academic landscape.

The Structure and Infrastructure of Academic Work

The structure and infrastructure of work shapes the nature of work and how well the work gets done. These elements are difficult to comprehend because they are typically not explicitly mentioned. However, it is essential that we appreciate their importance in academic work. Therefore, allow me to explain their significance in a physical context and then apply them to academic work.

In the physical sense, structure pertains to how space is allocated and arranged. When considering structure, one must first examine the goals and objectives of the work at hand. For instance, in the design of a house, an architect must determine the most important spaces and organize the house accordingly. Questions about priorities arise, such as whether to prioritize a large kitchen or a spacious master bedroom, or whether the bedrooms should be on the same floor or separate levels. The answers to these questions determine the allocation and arrangement of space. Once the structure is established, the architect must then consider the infrastructure systems necessary to support the functions of the structure.

Infrastructure in a home comprises the fundamental systems and organizational structures required to support the intended purpose of the structure. These systems include heating, air conditioning, electrical, plumbing, and more. Decisions regarding structure and infrastructure are inherently interconnected. For example, if a house will have multiple bathrooms, additional plumbing infrastructure will be necessary. Similarly, if a home audio and intercom system is desired, the electrical wiring infrastructure must be designed accordingly. It is critical that infrastructure decisions be made at the outset of a project, as retrofitting or modifying the infrastructure after construction is both costly and time-consuming. (Imagine a house needed to be rewired, replumbed or all the ductwork having to be redone after the house is completely built—Yikes!) By thoroughly contemplating the structure and infrastructure systems from the beginning, we can ensure that the finished product aligns with our goals.

Considering the necessary structure and infrastructure for a physical structure, such as a home, may seem relatively straightforward. However, as choice architects in education, determining the structure and infrastructure of our instructional design can be more challenging. Nonetheless, the same principles apply. In academic work, structure pertains to our priorities and is reflected in our actions and guidance provided to students during class time. Just as choice architecture theory posits, our choices directly impact the decisions students make regarding their academic work. For instance, if we simply review PowerPoint slides or lecture notes during class, students may conclude that they can forgo paying attention, thinking, "I can read them on my own." On the other hand, if we make the slides or notes available without reviewing them in class, students may mistake their absence as evidence that they are not important. The structure of work in this environment will differ depending on our priorities. I establish the structure of academic work by prioritizing the goals and objectives of instruction in a manner that ensures the fulfillment of the highest priorities and objectives. Thus, if my primary goal is for students to acquire a significant amount of accurate information, I may focus more on in-class activities. However, if my objective is to promote deep processing of information, I will design the course to promote learning away from class.

By recognizing the importance of structure and infrastructure in academic work, we can strategically shape the learning environment to align with our instructional goals. In addition to carefully considering the structure and infrastructure needs of our courses, we must also share these elements with students, just as architects discuss these elements with their clients. I and many other educators have used Figure S1.2 as a visual aid to help students comprehend the structural and infrastructure differences between high school and college.

From the second students register for classes, they unknowingly step into a structural trap. I vividly recall the sense of freedom students express during registration events when they realize that they will be in class less in college than they were in high school. At this early point in their college career,

High School vs. College Structural Comparison Chart

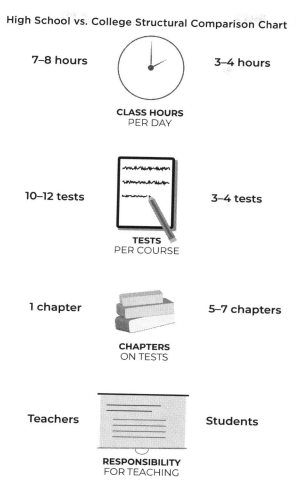

FIGURE S1.2   Illustration of four critical structural differences between high school and college environments, which serve as a starting point for our understanding

they can't imagine how quickly the sweet taste of independence will sour. However, the initial excitement of newfound independence quickly fades as they struggle to navigate their college environment with an outdated high school mindset. The structure and infrastructure of academic work in high school differs significantly from that in college, leaving students unprepared for the challenges they face. As teachers, we have the power to lay the groundwork for their success by adjusting our structure and providing the necessary infrastructure elements in our classrooms. To do so effectively, we must first understand how students experienced learning in high school, as highlighted by Paul Ramsden in *Learning to Teach in Higher Education* (Ramsden, 2005).

Continuous Schedule vs. Gapped Schedule

One major difference is the class schedule. In high school, students follow a continuous schedule. In this framework, students spend a considerable amount of time in class receiving instruction from their teachers. In this environment, students often have ample time to complete their work during school hours, which is a key regulatory benefit of the high school learning environment.

Did you know that college students are in class about half the time than they were in high school? This decrease amounts to an approximate fifty percent drop in direct instruction.

In college, the schedule is gapped, with classes scattered throughout the day and with breaks in between. For instance, instead of being in class continuously, students may have a class on Monday, Wednesday and Friday at 9:00 am–9:50 am, and then class from 11:00 am–11:50 am. Students may then have a break between 12:00 pm–3:00 pm, before ending their coursework for each day with a 3:00 pm lab session. I share a model for how successful students use the gapped scheduled framework to their benefit in the *Locus of Learning* chapter. However, at this point, you only need to understand that if students attempt to navigate the college schedule in the same way they did in high school, they will constantly feel that they do not have enough time to do quality work.

Timeline of Tests

Another difference lies in the timeline of tests. It's well known that students will have fewer tests and assessments in college (3–4) than they had in high school (10–12). However, have you ever deeply considered how fewer tests affect how students perceive and do academic work?

The decrease in the number of tests in college means that students will have fewer opportunities to recover from a poor test score. When you couple this fact with the common occurrence of initial poor performance, it is clear to see how students are put at a disadvantage early on. Adjusting to the reduced frequency and increased depth of learning required for spaced-out tests becomes essential.

Volume of Information

The volume of information is also significantly higher in college. Students must learn to efficiently process vast amounts of content right from the start of their college journey. This increase in information, coupled with the change in test distribution, is necessary for developing substantive knowledge demanded by college teachers. This factor will be covered in the *Cognitive Traps* section. At this point, you simply need to be aware that understanding and adapting to this sharp increase in information becomes crucial for students' success.

Responsibility for Teaching

Perhaps the most significant difference between high school and college lies in the responsibility for teaching. In high school, teachers regulate the learning process, providing structured activities and guiding students on a conveyor belt of academic work. However, in college, students are expected to learn independently. This shift from a dependent to an independent learning environment can be challenging for students, who may feel directionless and uncertain about what their college teachers expect. Students may suspect that "something" is different without the ability to precisely articulate the difference. Helping them understand and adapt to this change is vital for students' academic success.

When I share the structural differences that Figure S1.2 illustrates, students often experience a range of emotions, from frustration to a sense of enlightenment. Many are moved to tears. They express their emotions with statements such as, "Now, it all makes sense! I now realize why my hard work wasn't paying off!" Then, they become angry as they realize how avoidable their academic troubles were. Many retort, "Why didn't anyone tell us this in high school!" But once they understand the traps and learn ways to avoid them, they feel empowered and go on to have the successful college careers they crave. This book uncovers these transition traps and equips college teachers with the tools to help students navigate them.

It's important to note that college and high school teachers have different roles, aligned with the distinct outcomes of each educational level. However, students should be explicitly made aware of the differences between their previous and current learning environments, and college teachers should support them in transitioning to independent learners more effectively. By establishing new relationships between students and the college environment, teachers, and college-level work, colleges and universities can ensure a smoother transition for high school graduates. This process begins in the classroom.

In high school, the classroom functions as a regulated system, guiding students towards academic success through a structured schedule, infrastructure elements, and teacher-led activities. In contrast, the college classroom lacks such regulation, demanding that students take ownership of their learning. For this reason, it is crucial for us to help students understand what academic work entails and how to use the college structure to their advantage. By aligning our academic work structure with our priorities and implementing the necessary infrastructure components, we create a new workspace for students that helps them take ownership of their academic work.

Unfortunately, structural traps have become so commonplace in the educational landscape that many educators accept them as the norm. However, if you've heard the following sentiments at your institution, it's a clear indication that structural traps are present in your environment:

- "I struggle to find enough time to study." (student)
- "No matter how much effort I put in, my grades don't improve." (student)
- "I feel overwhelmed and undervalued." (faculty)
- "Our professional development initiatives aren't yielding significant results." (faculty or administrator)

These statements underscore the pervasiveness of structural traps and emphasize the urgency to acknowledge and address their impact on the teaching and learning experience.

2

WORKSPACE TRAP

Imagine yourself at an airport, strolling through the bustling terminal. As you navigate through the crowd, you come across a moving walkway—a conveyor belt designed to help passengers reach their destination faster and with less effort. You step onto the conveyor belt, and instantly you feel the smooth, gliding sensation as it propels you forward. It's a convenient and time-saving invention that many of us appreciate.

But have you ever wondered what it would be like to walk alongside the moving walkway? I have tested my speed walking ability and stamina by challenging those who are walking on the assisted walkway. I sometimes manage to beat them, though I must exert much more energy and effort than them. Perhaps when you have a bit more time on your hands, you can decide to test your own speed and stamina. You may win the race, but it will require more effort and energy on your part.

If you have used a moving walkway in the past, then you likely did not give much thought to the intricate pulley system operating beneath your feet. You likely remained largely unaware of the mechanics that made your journey easier and more enjoyable. The conveyor belt silently supported you, allowing you to reach your destination efficiently and effortlessly.

The high school classroom works a lot like a conveyor belt of learning for students. Teachers take on the role of the conveyor belt, guiding students through a carefully planned sequence of activities and interactions. By following this path, completing assigned work, and staying on track, students can be confident that they will acquire the necessary knowledge and succeed academically. It's a well-structured system that facilitates student success at the high school level.

DOI: 10.4324/9781003447252-3

To be clear, the high school classroom's conveyor belt model doesn't do the work *for* students, but it ensures that if they stay on track, following the prescribed sequence, they are likely to succeed. Just as the moving walkway aids passengers in reaching their destination faster with less effort, the structure and infrastructure of the high school classroom helps high school students achieve more with less effort. However, much like the hidden pulley system on the moving walkway, many students don't realize that their academic success is being supported by a well-oiled pulley system. Yet, these invisible forces pull students along, regulating their learning and increasing their likelihood of success.

It's not until students graduate from the conveyor-belt model of the high school classroom that they begin to realize that *something* crucial is missing. Without the familiar structure of the workspace and its accompanying infrastructure, they find themselves in a new academic environment—one where experimentation, regulation, and the assurance of proper learning are no longer guaranteed.

As college teachers, it's essential for us to understand the stark differences between the high school and college classroom experiences. Just as the conveyor belt model has its advantages in high school, the absence of the workspace in college classrooms can leave students feeling trapped. Many students have shared their observations, expressing a sense of something lacking in the college classroom. They struggle to articulate precisely what has changed, but they recognize the absence of the learning experience they once took for granted.

In the following sections of this chapter, we will delve deeper into the workspace and its multifaceted nature. We will examine how the workspace serves as both a structural component and an infrastructure system in high school classrooms, enabling students to test, adjust, and retest their hypotheses about their academic work. We will explore the labor associated with each regulatory role and shed light on the challenges students face when they enter the college classroom, ill-prepared for the absence of the workspace.

By understanding the importance of the workspace and its impact on students' learning experiences, we can reimagine our college classrooms and create environments that provide the necessary support and structure for our students to thrive. Together, let us embark on this journey of exploration and discovery, as we uncover the true significance of the workspace and its role in shaping our students' educational journeys.

The Workspace

The workspace plays two crucial roles in the high school classroom: it serves as both an essential structural feature and a critical infrastructure system for regulating student learning. Structurally, the workspace provides students and teachers with dedicated time and space to collaboratively engage with academic material. Functionally, the workspace is the specific segment of class time where students engage in important learning regulation tasks, enabling them to make meaningful contributions to their work. By "contributions," I am referring to students' ability to effectively convert the informational inputs they receive from teachers and other sources into tangible knowledge outcomes that will be assessed.

When observing high school classrooms, I've noticed a common practice: after the teacher covers the day's content, there is a designated period of time when the classroom transforms into a workspace for both students and teachers. While the teacher manages this workspace, its benefits are reaped by both parties. Students utilize the workspace to seek clarity, ensuring that their efforts will yield the knowledge that will be assessed. They receive valuable guidance and feedback from teachers, gaining insights into their existing knowledge and identifying areas where further growth is needed. During this segment of class time, students can exercise executive functions, such as redirecting their efforts when they veer off track, and they receive affirmation when they are on the right path. These benefits collectively enhance the effectiveness of students' work.

For teachers, the workspace serves as a platform for formative assessment of students' work, providing direction, feedback, and affirming their progress and understanding. It enables teachers to identify areas where students may be struggling, allowing them to tailor their instruction or adjust homework assignments accordingly. Perhaps most importantly, the workspace fosters alignment between teachers and students, facilitating a productive working relationship. The work carried out by students and teachers within the workspace serves as a fundamental infrastructure system, ensuring that students effectively regulate their learning and achieve the desired outcomes.

The workspace serves as a critical infrastructure system that allows students to test their hypotheses and experiment with various academic tasks. Throughout their academic journey, students constantly formulate hypotheses and conduct experiments, with test performance as the desired outcome they aim to control. However, since students cannot directly control their test performance (as grades are given by teachers), they focus on independent variables within their control. These variables encompass a range of academic tasks they undertake to improve their performance, such as notetaking, study time allocation, and study strategies. The workspace becomes the testing ground where students engage in experimentation, allowing them to adjust and refine their hypotheses.

Importantly, students are not alone in this experimentation process; their high school teachers are active participants in the workspace experiments. This collaboration is highly beneficial to students because teachers control the dependent variable they seek to influence: grades. Additionally, teachers also control another crucial variable that directly impacts grades, namely learning. They design the course, determine the necessary learning objectives, assess students' understanding, and assign grades. Their multifaceted roles as course designers, instructors, and assessors make their involvement in the workspace invaluable to students. This symbiotic relationship fosters a productive work environment.

Consider how the workspace aligns the work and regulation of work in the high school setting. Students, as active participants, engage in various academic activities, including class participation, homework completion, studying, and assessments. Teachers, on the other hand, regulate students' work by interconnecting content, instruction, activities, and assessments, ensuring that if students follow this structured path, they will learn and perform well. This alignment forms the bedrock of the workspace's significance as a fundamental structure in the high school classroom. It is the infrastructure system that guarantees the work students undertake yields the desired learning outcomes assessed through various evaluations. In essence, students simply need to commit to doing the work (a statement that gains new meaning in the Functional Traps chapter). As long as students are willing to be guided by their teachers, the activities and interactions within the workspace will greatly contribute to their success.

However, in the college classroom, the workspace and its rich work and regulatory benefits are notably absent. It comes as no surprise that students can feel trapped in this new environment. Jericho, a freshman student at Gonzaga University in 2020, aptly compared the instructional models of high school and college, stating,

> In high school, the teacher introduces the material, then guides us through it before summarizing what the lesson was about. But in college, many of my professors teach until the class time is up. They don't end the lesson; they just stop, and we leave.

Many students share similar observations, realizing that a certain learning experience they took for granted in high school is missing from college instruction. Without the workspace, students are unable to engage in effective experimentation and are left to chance, hoping that what they learn aligns with what will be assessed.

Workspace Assessment

To determine if your classroom fosters a workspace environment similar to those students experienced in high school, consider the following questions:

- Do you take responsibility for helping students align their learning with assessments?

- Do you assign specific homework tasks to students?
- Do you strategically incorporate students' homework assignments into your instruction?
- Do you provide students with test reviews that closely resemble the upcoming assessments?

If you answered "yes" to these questions, it is likely that you are providing a workspace for your students. However, it is important to note that most college teachers answer "no" to most or all of these questions, implicitly expecting students to take on these regulatory roles themselves. The Division of Labor Traps chapter will delve further into the labor associated with each regulatory role. For now, consider the academic work experience of students without the familiar workspace they relied upon in the past. It becomes a situation of the blind leading the blind, and the harder students work, the more they find themselves trapped.

While emphasizing the significance of the workspace, it is essential to acknowledge that it is not the sole component of high school instruction. It is one component, strategically positioned as the penultimate stage in the class sequence, precisely serving its regulatory function. To fully comprehend the workspace's role as a regulator, let us examine a typical high school classroom lesson.

The High School Classroom

Based on my extensive observations of high school classrooms and interactions with students throughout North America, I'm fully aware of the significant variations in high school classroom instruction across the continent. Consequently, I acknowledge the inherent risk in attempting to provide a universal model of high school instruction that encompasses each student's experience. Nevertheless, while instructional approaches may differ, they typically follow a three-phase structure: a clear beginning, middle, and end (Drexel University, 2021). During focus group discussions, students often acknowledge this pattern and note the contrasting dynamics they encounter in college classrooms. Recall Jericho's comparison of the differences between how her high school and college lessons unfolded.

> In high school, the teacher introduces the material, then guides us through it before summarizing what the lesson was about. But in college, many of my professors teach until the class time is up. They don't end the lesson; they just stop, and we leave.

Jericho fondly recalls the introduction, guidance, and summarization that resemble the breakdown of a high school teacher's lesson on the foundations and functions of government in a government and civics course.

Beginning

The initial phase involves contextualization. In Stage 1 of the BDP (Backward Design Process), teachers establish a clear desired result that sets the course for their instruction. Through conversations with high school teachers, instructional leaders, and administrators, I have learned that this desired result encompasses a synthesis of state, local, and personal standards. For the foundations and function of government lesson, this synthesized outcome might be presented to students in the following statement: "You will understand the historical development and current status of the fundamental concepts and processes of authority, power, and influence, with particular emphasis on the democratic skills and attitudes necessary to become responsible citizens." This statement establishes the boundaries of the course and serves as an essential framework for effective teaching and learning. However, in my experience, this statement is often used merely as an introductory statement for students and as a checklist item at the end of the course. Nonetheless, the teacher begins with the end in mind, as proposed by the BDP, and this statement becomes a conceptual map guiding their instruction throughout the course.

Connect

The second step that high school teachers take is to help students establish coherence across multiple class sessions. In this example, the teacher might explicitly connect the current lesson to prior work, saying something like,

> In the last class, we summarized amendments one through five in the same manner, and you were assigned a specific amendment, by group, to analyze and break down according to key vocabulary, with each part explained in simple terms and with modern-day applications/issues related to each amendment.

By fusing these connections to broader course goals, the teacher enhances the likelihood of students linking the daily content together, instead of perceiving each day's material in isolation. The teacher may even pose an essential question, such as, "What are the specific powers of both the House of Representatives and the Senate?"

By contextualizing the course and facilitating content connections, high school teachers assist students in regulating their learning. Although students might not realize it at the time, they are essentially on a conveyor belt, with their teacher actively pulling them along. This sense of guidance and support, as reminisced by Jericho, emerged during the focus group session.

Middle

Direct instruction constitutes the core of this phase, during which the teacher delivers the day's content. The extent of direct instruction time varies depending on the teacher's style, ranging from lectures lasting most of the time to shorter content coverage of around 10 to 20 minutes. However, the transformative aspect of the class occurs after the content delivery, as the classroom transforms into a workspace.

The workspace plays a crucial role in regulating the high school classroom environment. It provides time and space for guided activities, independent work, reflection, and adjustments. Within this workspace, the teacher assumes a vital role as the agent leading students through guided activities, helping them navigate and comprehend complex information. The teacher monitors students' application of knowledge and skills, identifies errors in understanding, and gathers insights into their processing and comprehension of the material. In focus groups I conducted with college students, many participants fondly recalled their high school teachers actively scouring the room, proactively checking on their progress. Teachers would spend a few minutes observing students, engaging in deeper discussions, assisting with problem-solving, or helping students develop ideas for papers or speeches. These teacher-led efforts serve as mechanisms that propel students forward on the conveyor belt towards success. Moreover, the workspace also benefits teachers by providing a wealth of data on how their students work and learn.

In addition to facilitating student learning regulation, the workspace offers invaluable opportunities for teachers to closely observe students as they engage with the material. This empathic observation of students actively working on the assigned tasks provides valuable formative data, helping identify areas where students may be struggling, heading in the wrong direction, or in need of clarification. Typically, high school students lack the necessary self-regulation skills to manage their learning, as noted by (Hall, 2004). Consequently, when they encounter academic challenges, they often misinterpret the situation and may invest effort in the wrong direction, study incorrect material, or study with the wrong outcomes in mind (Kelemen, 2000). Without the teachers' observations, students would likely continue on the wrong path or become frustrated by their inability to grasp certain concepts, potentially leading to giving up. However, with teachers assuming the role of learning managers, students benefit from corrective actions. Nevertheless, these benefits come at the expense of students developing their own learning regulation skills, which are crucial for success in college.

While observing high school classrooms, I am constantly assessing the division of labor, scrutinizing who is responsible for what tasks inside and outside the classroom. In most cases, teachers bear the brunt of the heavy lifting. For instance, in the foundations and functions of government class, it is often the teacher who recognizes that students struggle to differentiate between authority, power, and influence within a democratic society. Such observations prompt the teacher to revisit the board or take control of the screen to clarify these concepts. This clarification saves students from wasting time and effort pursuing incorrect learning paths, while also providing teachers with valuable insights that allow them to make on-the-spot instructional adjustments or assign homework more strategically. This work carried out by the teacher is commendable, but it is crucial for students to develop similar skills to thrive in college.

Independent Activity

Subsequently, the teacher may allocate time for students to work on their assignments in class. For example, students could be asked to choose from various assignments, such as:

- Assignment A: Using graphic organizers and Venn diagrams, depict the powers of the House and the Senate.
- Assignment B: Research the demographics of members of Congress, including data on median age, youngest and eldest members, numbers of women, racial minorities, etc., who make up the House/Senate.
- Assignment C: Complete an Edpuzzle (videos with embedded questions) about Congress.

Given that students have been working throughout the class, diligent and proficient learners, such as Kareem, may complete their work before leaving.

End

In this phase, teachers often engage in micro-formal assessments to gauge students' knowledge and skills, typically through quizzes or tests. This step allows teachers to evaluate the sufficiency of students' learning in relation to their instructional objectives, which only the teacher has in mind. Additionally, these assessments provide teachers with post-work data, while allowing students to accumulate low-stakes grades. Sample quiz questions might include:

1 The Speaker of the House

    a Is the most powerful officer in Congress.

    b Is appointed by the president.

c Must belong to the same political party as the president.
d Cannot be elected to more than two consecutive terms.

2 To ensure that the majority of all senators are experienced,

a Junior senators are elected for eight-year terms.
b Only one-third of the senators are up for reelection every two years.
c Senior senators chair all committees.
d All senators are guaranteed two terms in office.

3 The Senate, unlike the House of Representatives, does not have the power to

a Pass laws regulating trade.
b Introduce appropriation bills.
c Try impeached officials.
d Approve treaties.

Closure

To close the lesson out, the teacher may summarize the main points for students or lead them in a closing activity that helps them consolidate the key concepts. As a final act, the teacher may assign specific tasks as homework, such as answering a set of questions about Representatives and Senators using links to relevant websites or writing a letter to their Representative or one of their Senators, addressing a particular issue related to the country or government.

As illustrated, the high school workspace serves as a vital component of the conveyor belt classroom model. The intricate network of activities, monitoring, and management functions act as a pulley system that enables teachers to regulate much of the learning process for students. If students remain on the conveyor belt and actively participate, success is almost guaranteed. Even an average student would have to deliberately avoid participating to evade learning the material.

Due to the comprehensive learning regulation provided by teachers, low performance and failure often result from deliberate acts of omission, such as students actively avoiding their assigned work. To fail, students must intentionally jump off the moving conveyor belt. If students follow the sequence of sessions and activities, they not only learn the specific material covered but also develop a strong understanding of how they will be assessed on that material. However, as we will soon see, this dynamic poses significant challenges for students when they transition to college.

The conveyor belt classroom model is suitable for high school, where teachers bear responsibility for student performance without control over what students do outside their classrooms. I am not here to pass judgment on whether the high school system is good or bad. What I have observed is its incompatibility with the independent learner model required in college.

Creating a College Workspace

As educators, our ultimate goal is to nurture independent learners among our college students. However, achieving this objective poses significant challenges. To become independent learners, students require a well-defined work process that facilitates the conversion of informational inputs into assessed outcomes. There are three essential elements that students need to cultivate their independence:

1 a comprehensive understanding of the informational ingredients necessary for knowledge production
2 knowledge of the cognitive interactions required to achieve desired outcomes, and
3 a suitable workspace for their work.

In the following sections, I will delve into each of these elements, with a particular focus on cognitive interactions in the dedicated section on Cognitive Traps.

In the preceding section, we established that the high school workspace allows students to complete their work during class time and still be adequately prepared for assessments, often without significant efforts beyond the classroom. This model works well in the high school structure due to how the academic work formula us applied (Figure 2.1). As a reminder, academic work follows a simple equation.

This formula provides students with a practical framework applicable to any course. However, the primary challenge for college students lies not in learning the inputs of academic work, but rather in converting the inputs into appropriate outcomes, and we, as educators, bear partial responsibility for their lack of success. To enable students to navigate these challenges and function as competent independent learners, we must provide them specific information. Crucially, this information can be delivered through our syllabi, offering guidance and support to help students avoid structural traps and foster their independence.

$$\text{Inputs} + \text{Processing} = \text{Outcomes}$$

FIGURE 2.1   Academic work formula.

Now, let us explore how we can transform the traditional view of the syllabus and harness its potential as a powerful tool to create an effective workspace for independent learning. By utilizing the syllabus strategically and communicating the outcomes upfront, while also developing and using key infrastructure elements that I call metacognitive learning outcomes, we can empower students to take control of their learning journey, bridge the gap between high school and college expectations, and succeed as independent learners.

Step 1) To Create a Workspace, Use Your Syllabus as a Tool

Many college teachers view their syllabus as a mere document, primarily created for administrative purposes or to satisfy higher authorities. Unfortunately, this limited perspective becomes evident as the course progresses, with the syllabus rarely revisited beyond the initial days. However, when conceived and constructed thoughtfully, the syllabus can provide students with valuable information to effectively engage in academic work. Authors O'Brien and Cohen, in their book *The Course Syllabus* (O'Brien & Cohen, 2008), highlight how elements within a syllabus can serve as regulatory devices, helping students understand the course's direction and monitor their progress towards learning objectives.

Another valuable approach is Mary Ann Winkelmes' Transparency in Learning and Teaching (TILT) method (Winkelmes, 2013), which emphasizes the explicit communication of expectations and the clarification of implicit elements in academic work. This method demonstrates that faculty can significantly enhance student learning and performance by making expectations transparent. By connecting daily course content and activities to the overall purpose of the course, students gain a sense of purpose and coherence across multiple classes. This combination of purposefulness and coherence enables students to engage in essential regulatory skills such as planning, monitoring, and evaluating their learning. To unlock these benefits, we must shift our perception of the syllabus from a static document to a dynamic tool.

Step 2) To Create a Workspace, Communicate the Outcomes Upfront

In the Backward Design Process, effective college teachers understand the significance of considering the end goals at the beginning of the design sequence. Similarly, students must also begin with the end in mind. However, the meaning of knowing the end upfront differs between high school and college.

In high school, the outcomes of academic work tend to closely resemble the inputs received in class or from course sources. This similarity allows students to produce outcomes using relatively low cognitive effort. For instance, imagine a high school government and civics course where students are provided detailed notes on the foundations and functions of government as the inputs. Two weeks later, the teacher assigns a paper on the same topic, as the knowledge product. In this case, students can simply study the notes, store them in their minds, and review them while writing the paper. When the inputs and outcomes align closely, the workspace becomes highly effective, even if students did not have the end in mind during their exposure to the inputs. Understanding this type of learning experience is crucial for college teachers, as it has significant implications for how students approach their work in college.

In contrast, college-level outcomes often require higher-level cognitive skills to transform the inputs into the desired outcomes. Simply studying notes for hours or days may not adequately prepare students to produce excellent work when the outcomes differ qualitatively from the inputs. Students need to know the outcomes upfront, especially when they deviate from the inputs, to operate as independent learners successfully. Without this key informational ingredient, students may struggle to contribute effectively to the work required for the desired outcomes. This is where Metacognitive Learning Outcomes (MLOs) play a vital role.

Step 3) To Create a Workspace, Develop Metacognitive Learning Outcomes

To empower students to convert course content into meaningful knowledge products, they need metacognitive learning outcomes. These outcomes serve as tools that provide students with the necessary information to regulate their learning effectively. Academic work is a collaborative effort between students and teachers, with each stakeholder making distinct contributions to the knowledge-making process. While teachers control the inputs by shaping classroom instruction and providing resources, students take charge of the process of producing the outcomes, primarily outside the classroom.

As depicted in Figure 2.2, not all MLOs are created equal. It is recommended that faculty incorporate all six components shown in the "best" column when developing metacognitive learning outcomes. These comprehensive tools offer students the clarity and direction they need to manage their learning effectively. Since educators cannot predict every student's academic deficiency, MLOs provide the informational ingredients necessary for

Good	Better	Best
1. Outcomes accurately express the core knowledge products students must produce.	1. Outcomes accurately express the core knowledge products students must produce.	1. Outcomes accurately express the core knowledge products students must produce.
2. Outcomes are hierarchically organized.	2. Outcomes are hierarchically organized.	2. Outcomes are hierarchically organized.
3. Outcomes are specific and action-oriented.	3. Outcomes are specific and action-oriented.	3. Outcomes are specific and action-oriented.
4. Outcomes are limited to no more than eight.	4. Outcomes are limited to no more than eight.	4. Outcomes are limited to no more than eight.
	5. Outcomes include the respective thinking skills needed to produce the knowledge product.	5. Outcomes include the respective thinking skills needed to produce the knowledge product.
		6. The method of demonstration is included.

Requires greater managing-up skills ⟷ Requires less managing-up skills

FIGURE 2.2 Metacognitive learning outcome (MLO) rubric.

students to regulate their learning. Including multiple components in the learning outcomes reduces the burden on students to manage their learning independently and increases their chances of successfully mastering the material.

By recognizing the potential of the syllabus as a tool, communicating the outcomes upfront, and providing metacognitive learning outcomes, college teachers can create a workspace that fosters independent learning among students. These steps help students avoid workspace traps and empower students to take ownership of their academic work and regulate their learning.

Metacognitive Learning Outcomes (MLOs) serve as crucial infrastructure elements for students to engage in academic work due to three primary reasons:

1 *Direction and Destination:* Metacognitive Learning Outcomes (MLOs) serve as essential infrastructure elements in academic work by providing students with a clear direction for their thinking and serving as the

destination for their learning. When students understand the desired outcomes upfront, they can align their efforts and focus on producing the course outcomes they aim to achieve. This empowers them to navigate through the daily course content with a purpose, knowing how to utilize the information to generate the desired outcomes effectively.

2 *Long-Term Perspective:* MLOs evoke a long-term perspective, enabling students to remain focused on the future course outcomes while effectively working with the inputs in the present. Research consistently shows a strong correlation between a long time perspective and success. By holding MLOs in mind throughout their learning journey, students develop the ability to make better decisions in the present, aligning their actions with their long-term goals. This shift in perspective enhances their capacity to prioritize tasks and allocate their time and resources effectively.

3 *Outcome-Oriented Assessment:* MLOs fundamentally transform the assessment process by enabling students to evaluate their work based on the outcomes they produce rather than solely on the time or effort invested. This shift in assessment methodology promotes a deeper understanding of the subject matter and encourages students to focus on the quality of their outcomes. By emphasizing outcome-oriented assessment, MLOs create a framework that fosters critical thinking and application of knowledge, as students are motivated to achieve the desired outcomes rather than merely completing tasks.

To illustrate the significance of MLOs, let's consider an example. Imagine students taking a literature course where they are required to read five short poems by different authors. Without knowledge of the specific learning outcome, such as "writing a paper illustrating how each author used symbolism," students may overlook the intended purpose of their reading. They may have instead used their energy to develop accurate recollections of each poem, which is not what was being assessed. However, if they start with a clear understanding of the outcome, they can approach the poems with the end goal of analyzing symbolism in mind. This aligns their reading experience with the desired assessment and ensures they acquire the necessary inputs to produce the expected outcomes.

As another example of the impact of MLOs, I recall observing a group of students studying for a course titled "Accounting for Decision Making." In this course, students were required to read various financial filings and corporate disclosures filed with the Securities Exchange Commission. Without knowledge of the specific learning outcome, such as "making decisions based on the information gleaned from the financial filings," students meticulously studied the documents without understanding their purpose. They learned the details of each document, but they missed the essence of the course, which was to sharpen their ability to make informed decisions with the information. In this case, the difference between focusing on the details of financial filings and utilizing that information to make decisions is significant. Students' inability to bridge this gap prevents them from achieving the intended learning outcome, resulting in their performance falling short despite their efforts.

By incorporating MLOs into the course, the professor can transform the learning experience for students. With the revised learning statements focusing on MLOs, such as "utilizing information from financial filings to make informed decisions" and "demonstrating critical analysis skills in interpreting corporate disclosures," students are now equipped with a clear understanding of the desired outcomes. This shift enables students to connect the discrete course inputs to the broader, longer-term learning outcomes, allowing them to bridge the gap between knowledge acquisition and practical application. The adoption of MLOs empowers students to approach their learning with purpose, ensuring they acquire the necessary inputs and skills to produce the expected outcomes and achieve success in their academic journey.

Furthermore, MLOs play a vital role in promoting independent learning, a crucial aspect of academic success outside the classroom. It's inevitable that students will encounter gaps in their knowledge, things they simply were not exposed to previously. These gaps can become major obstacles for students.

Independent learning requires students to overcome knowledge gaps and acquire new information efficiently. MLOs address these challenges by providing students with the necessary tools and guidance to bridge those gaps and expedite their learning process.

Cheryl, a student at a university in the midwest, experienced firsthand the consequences of not having a clear understanding of the learning outcomes. As a graduate of an under-resourced, inner-city high school, she often felt disadvantaged compared to college classmates. However, Cheryl's determination to overcome her challenges remained unwavering. It wasn't until her physical chemistry professor updated her traditional learning statements to metacognitive learning outcomes that Cheryl found a way to overcome of knowledge gaps and unlock her full potential.

The following table compares her professor's old and new course statements.

Former Course Goals	*New Metacognitive Learning Outcomes*
1.1. Hands-on practice applying physical chemistry* to multiple chemical and biochemical systems. *What is physical chemistry? A fascination with how the structure of atoms and molecules control the behavior and reactivity of bulk matter.	1. Decode the fundamental laws, theories, and postulates central to physical chemistry by describing how an example or practice problem illustrates a specific law, theory, or postulate in concept checks and conceptual test problems.
1.1.1. An increased ability to apply models and equations based on fundamental laws of thermodynamics and to use these results to interpret molecular behavior.	2. Apply correct equations for obtained/provided data in numerical practice, problem set, and text questions to predict a system's final conditions and/or a reaction mixture's composition.
1.1.2. A deeper proficiency to describe factors controlling the rate of reactions mathematically.	3. Evaluate a model's description of data to determine assumptions inherent in the data or the model through lab calculations and written lab discussions and through interpretation of numerical problems.
1.1.3. A working knowledge of the fundamental tools, concepts, and models of quantum chemistry that describe how atoms and molecules interact with electromagnetic radiation.	4. Infer atomic/molecular level interactions from agreement between measured macroscopic values and predicted values of idealized systems through lab calculations and written lab discussions and through interpretation of numerical problems.
1.1.4. An appreciation of the power and universality of statistical mechanics.	5. Synthesize multiple experiments from several research groups addressing the rate(s) of change of specific molecules using chemical/biochemical kinetics through a literature review paper.
1.2. The exploration of the connection between fundamental theories (often summarized in powerful equations) and intriguing applications (described in the chemical and biochemical literature).	
1.3. Heightened critical thinking and problem-solving skills practiced individually and in a team.	
1.4. Further exposure to reading and interpreting chemical and biochemical literature.	
1.5. An increased ability to collect and then succinctly and precisely communicate scientific results.	

Unlike her classmates, Cheryl didn't recall being taught the fundamental laws, theories, and postulates of physical chemistry. Her professor assumed that students already possessed this knowledge, leaving Cheryl feeling unprepared and lost.

However, Cheryl's determination and resourcefulness led her to find a solution. During the focus group, she shared her strategy for acing the course despite her initial under-preparedness. She relied on the MLOs provided in the course to identify the necessary informational ingredients. When she realized that the class content didn't cover what she needed, Cheryl took matters into her own hands. She utilized an online chemistry textbook to learn the missing material, effectively creating her own workspace to bridge the knowledge gap.

With the revised course statements emphasizing MLOs, Cheryl gained a newfound clarity and direction for her learning. She realized that her initial struggles were not solely due to her educational background but also stemmed from a lack of explicit guidance and clear outcomes. MLOs provided Cheryl with the necessary tools to properly construct her knowledge. They enabled her to identify the inputs she needed to focus on, understand how to process that information, and connect it to the desired long-term outcomes.

Armed with this transformative approach, Cheryl embraced her studies with renewed purpose. She began to utilize MLOs as guiding tools, constantly keeping the desired outcomes in mind as she accumulated knowledge and worked on various tasks. Cheryl's dedication and strategic approach paid off as she bridged the knowledge gaps she once faced. She not only caught up with her peers but also surpassed their knowledge base, showcasing the effectiveness of MLOs in promoting independent learning and overcoming initial disadvantages.

Cheryl's experience serves as a poignant example of the importance of updating course statements to incorporate MLOs. Without clear learning outcomes, students like Cheryl would be left to navigate the course without guidance or support. They would either hope to succeed without the necessary material or continually rely on their teachers during office hours for remedial instruction.

Recalling a particularly disheartening moment, Cheryl shared how a different professor questioned her suitability for a science major due to her frequent visits to office hours for re-teaching. This lack of clarity and guidance left Cheryl unsure of what she needed to do with the information she was acquiring. She found herself gathering inputs without a clear purpose, storing them in her mental warehouse without knowing how to utilize them effectively.

However, with the introduction of MLOs, Cheryl experienced a transformative shift in her learning approach. The MLOs provided her with a clear roadmap, enabling her to strategically use the given inputs and engage in additional work to build up her knowledge. This empowered Cheryl to level the playing field between herself and her peers, bridging the gaps in her understanding and demonstrating her capability in the subject.

Cheryl's story emphasizes the crucial role of MLOs in empowering students to take control of their learning and overcome challenges. By incorporating MLOs, educators can provide students with the direction, clarity, and purpose they need to succeed. MLOs ensure that students like Cheryl have a roadmap to guide their learning, enabling them to make informed decisions, leverage available resources, and reach their full potential.

As you can see, Metacognitive Learning Outcomes (MLOs) are invaluable tools for college students, equipping them with the essential informational ingredients required to excel in their academic work. MLOs serve as a fundamental infrastructure element that empowers students to work effectively within their designated workspace.

Create Your Own MLOs

You can convert your current learning statements to MLOs or create MLOs by turning the rubric criteria into questions.

1 *Do your outcomes reflect the core knowledge products students must produce?*

This initial step can be challenging for many teachers as it requires us to crystallize the desired end "products" we aim for our students to achieve. Take a holistic view of your course and consider dividing this process into the following three categories.

Knowledge	*Skill*	*Knowledge and Skill*
What should students know at the end of this course?	What should students be able to do at the end of this course?	What will students know and be able to do when this course is over?

2 *Are your outcomes hierarchically organized?*

Academic knowledge typically follows a progression from basic information to more complex concepts. Hence, when crafting your outcomes, strive to arrange them in a logical order, starting with those that students are likely to produce first and progressing accordingly.

3 *Are your outcomes specific and action-oriented?*

As MLOs serve as instructional products, they should direct students to take specific actions. Use precise verbs that convey the cognitive skills students must employ to process the inputs effectively. We will explore the cognitive element in greater detail in the Cognitive Traps section.

4 *Do you have eight or fewer outcomes?*

It is common for teachers to generate more outcomes than necessary. To maintain clarity and focus, I recommend keeping the number of outcomes to a maximum of eight.

5 *Do your outcomes connect the cognitive labor that students must enact on the course content to produce the appropriate level of outcomes?*

Academic outcomes are the result of students employing their mental faculties to transform inputs into outcomes. Well-conceived MLOs must explicitly convey the skills required for each respective outcome. Avoid using vague filler words like "demonstrate" or "understand" that fail to precisely express the necessary skills. We will delve into determining the precise cognitive skills in the Cognitive Traps section.

6 *Do your outcomes tell students how they will be assessed?*

To enable students to study effectively, they need to know in advance how their knowledge will be evaluated. By aligning their studying with the assessment methods, students can better prepare themselves.

By implementing MLOs, both teachers and students benefit. Students can engage in high-quality academic work with minimal need for reteaching, which ultimately reduces the burden on teachers.

In summary, MLOs serve as indispensable tools for students, providing them with the necessary informational ingredients for academic success. By creating well-structured and thoughtful MLOs, teachers can empower students to excel, fostering a productive learning environment.

MLO Activity

Review the outcomes below and determine which criterion is missing. We will leave out component number two and four because they can only be determined by reviewing the entire list of outcomes.

Single Outcome Example #1 (Cake Baking and Construction): Blank

Course Cake Baking and Construction	Outcome The student will produce different types of dough and cake such as classic dacquoise, genoise, and sponge to use in creating their celebration cakes.

MLO Components	Yes or No
1. Outcomes accurately reflect the core knowledge products students must produce.	
3. Outcomes are specific and action oriented.	
5. Outcomes include the respective thinking skills needed to produce the knowledge product.	
6. Outcomes include the method of demonstration.	

Single Outcome Example #1 (Cake Baking and Construction): Answer key

Course Cake Baking and Construction	Outcome The student will produce different types of dough and cake such as classic dacquoise, genoise, and sponge to use in creating their celebration cakes.

MLO Components	Yes or No
2. Outcomes accurately reflect the core knowledge products students must produce.	Yes
3. Outcomes are specific and action oriented.	Yes
5. Outcomes include the respective thinking skills needed to produce the knowledge product.	Yes
7. Outcomes include the method of demonstration.	Yes

Single Outcome Example #1 (Cake Baking and Construction): Explanation

Course Cake Baking and Construction	Outcome The student will produce different types of dough and cake such as classic dacquoise, genoise, and sponge to use in creating their celebration cakes.
MLO Components	Yes or No
3. Outcomes accurately reflect the core knowledge products students must produce.	Yes This outcome certainly provides students a product that is central to the course.
3. Outcomes are specific and action oriented.	Yes This outcome informs students what they must use in their cake construction and references examples.
5. Outcomes include the respective thinking skills needed to produce the knowledge product.	Yes While this outcome doesn't explicitly include a cognitive skill, the thinking skill is less important because students are making a physical object.
8. Outcomes include the method of demonstration.	Yes This outcome is implied since students are making a physical object. However, if there were other potential ways of expressing the outcome, such as digital display, then it should be explicitly expressed.

There is little doubt that if students implant this outcome in their minds, then they will know that the knowledge they gain about dough and cakes must ultimately be used to create a celebration cake that fits the explicated criteria.

Single Outcome Example #2 (history/African American history course): Blank

Course	Outcome
History	To think and write critically within the discipline of history.

MLO Components	Yes or No
4. Outcomes accurately reflect the core knowledge products students must produce.	
3. Outcomes are specific and action oriented.	
5. Outcomes include the respective thinking skills needed to produce the knowledge product.	
9. Outcomes include the method of demonstration.	

Single Outcome Example #2 (history/African American history course): Answer

Course	Outcome
History	To think and write critically within the discipline of history.

MLO Components	Yes or No
Outcomes accurately reflect the core knowledge products students must produce.	No. This outcome is too broad for students to use as an effective guide or gauge for their learning.
Outcomes are specific and action oriented.	No. "think and write critically" are neither specific cognitive behaviors or actionable.
Outcomes include the respective thinking skills needed to produce the knowledge product.	No. "think" and "critically" are too generic of terms. They won't be of much use to students.
Outcomes include the method of demonstration.	No. This outcome does not inform students how they must demonstrate their knowledge.

Single Outcome Example #2 (history/African American history course): Rewrite

Course History	Outcome **Explain** the impact and legacy of nationalism and colonialism on economic, social, and political relationships and institutions in Africa, Europe, Asia, and the Americas.
MLO Components	Yes or No
Outcomes accurately reflect the core knowledge products students must produce.	Yes This outcome expresses a significant knowledge product for students.
Outcomes are specific and action oriented.	Yes Students know that they must know how nationalism and colonialism impacted the economic, social, and political relationships and institutions of the continents listed.
Outcomes include the respective thinking skills needed to produce the knowledge product.	Yes Students are foretold that they must "explain," which connotes a specific mode of thinking.
Outcomes include the method of demonstration.	No This outcome could be strengthened by sharing how students must express their knowledge, such as in a group presentation, paper, or storyboard.
Even though this rewrite is missing the method of demonstration, it provides students better guidance for their work and serves as a better gauge of their learning than the original outcome. This is a useful tool for students to use in their workspace frame of mind to construct their knowledge.	

In conclusion, MLOs serve as crucial infrastructure devices that empower students to self-regulate their learning. They do not make academic work inherently easier, but rather, they simplify the process by eliminating unnecessary complications. The inclusion of comprehensive components in MLOs reduces the energy and effort students would otherwise spend in trying to decipher teachers' expectations. As a result, students can allocate more time and focus towards producing high-quality academic work.

Students rely on MLOs within their workspace as these devices enable them to effectively plan how to utilize the inputs, monitor their thinking throughout the learning process, and evaluate their outcomes before teachers do. This self-inspection ensures that the knowledge they produce aligns with the knowledge that will be assessed, minimizing frustration for both students and educators.

In essence, MLOs act as indispensable tools that facilitate students' ability to navigate their academic journey with clarity and purpose. By incorporating MLOs, we can create a conducive learning environment where students can optimize their efforts and achieve meaningful academic outcomes.

The Workspace in Action

During my consulting visits, I often have the opportunity to observe classes in session and engage with students afterward to gain insights into their understanding of the lesson. As students exit the class, while the information is still fresh in their minds, I inquire about their perception of what the class was about. When I ask students to summarize what the class was about, I get several different answers. Educators are often bewildered by students' interpretations.

For instance, during my observation of a calculus course at an engineering university, the professors used examples of a hot air balloon and a dump truck to teach the concept of related rates. However, while the professors' intention was to impart the understanding of related rates, many students believed that the primary objective was to memorize the formulas used to solve the specific problems involving the hot air balloon and dump truck.

It should not come as a shock that college educators encounter such divergent interpretations of their lessons. In high school, students were not responsible for discerning the purpose of their lessons; it was done for them in the workspace by their teachers. Furthermore, they did not have to contextualize information or make connections across various courses, as their teachers' regulatory regimes took care of that in the workspace. Consequently, it is not surprising that students struggle to derive purpose and establish coherence across multiple classes when this regulatory function is absent.

With the regulatory mechanisms that guided students' work and learning in high school now absent from the college classroom, students are left to regulate their own learning. However, research suggests that their self-regulatory abilities are often insufficient (Hall, 2004, Kelemen, 2000). This is where MLOs come into play as the necessary GPS device for students, providing clarity on what they need to know and identifying any knowledge gaps between their current understanding and the knowledge required for upcoming assessments. MLOs offer the informational context students need to effectively process the course content.

Upon examining the professor's learning outcomes, I found the following statement on page three of the course syllabus: "Students must be able to use the chain rule to find the rate of change of one quantity that depends on the rate of change of other quantities." Although the term "related rates" was not explicitly mentioned in this learning outcome, its inclusion is not crucial. It is impractical to expressly include every concept in a learning outcome, particularly when aiming to limit the total number of outcomes to eight or fewer. However, "related rates" did appear twice elsewhere in the syllabus. I have underlined its presence in a list of topics on page six of the syllabus.

6 Chapter 3: Differentiation Rules
3.1 Derivatives of Polynomials and Exponential Functions
3.2 The Product and Quotient Rules
3.3 Derivatives of Trigonometric Functions
3.4 The Chain Rule
3.5 Implicit Differentiation
3.6 Derivatives of Logarithmic Functions
3.7 Rates of Change in Natural and Social Sciences
3.8 Optional: Exponential Growth and Decay
3.9 Related Rates
3.10 Linear Approximations and Differentials
3.11 Optional: Hyperbolic Functions

In addition to embedding the concept of related rates among other associated concepts, page seven of the syllabus also includes a timeline and sequence indicating when this topic will be taught.

7	3.4 The chain rule
(Feb 15–21)	3.5 Implicit differentiation
	3.6 Derivatives of inverse functions and logarithms
7	3.7 Derivative of Rate of Change
(Feb 22–28)	3.9 Related rates
	3.9 Related rates
8	3.10 Linearization/Approximation
(Mar 1–7)	Chapter 4. Applications of Derivatives
	4.1 Max and Min Value

As I have observed in numerous courses, I was genuinely impressed by the well-structured syllabi. However, I noticed that the professor treated it merely as a document rather than a tool. The syllabus was covered briefly in the first class and rarely referred to again. Similarly, once students took note of important details like the attendance policy, testing dates, and grading scale, they seldom revisited the syllabus. Yet, if utilized as a tool, the syllabus could greatly enhance students' learning experience, making the work more efficient and meaningful learning more achievable.

When the syllabus is used as a tool, students can utilize the information on page six regarding the progression of topics and the interrelationships among those closely associated with related rates on page seven to construct their knowledge. Recognizing that the issue of students focusing solely on solving specific examples rather than understanding concepts persisted in math and math-related courses, I proposed a slight innovation in the classroom to incorporate a workspace.

First, I suggested that all courses incorporate the following macro course outcome:

> Students must be able to apply their knowledge and cognitive skills to solve problems they cannot predict in contexts they do not know in advance.

The development of this outcome was based on comparing the mental efforts of successful students to those who were less successful. While observing students working away from class, I noticed qualitative differences between how successful and unsuccessful students worked. After observing several classes and understanding the dynamics within, I realized that successful students attained a deep level of comprehension of the course concepts. When studying, they sought to grasp the chain rule, derivatives, related rates, and other abstract concepts. They then used this conceptual understanding to determine which computational methods to employ and ultimately work through the problems. Their conceptual grasp enabled them to approach problems differently than their less successful peers, who often put in more effort. I witnessed a deep approach to learning in action, as I had anticipated from my research.

Conversely, less successful students took a surface approach to learning, skipping over the concepts taught in class and focusing solely on individual problems. After class, their objective was to learn how to solve those specific problems, expecting to encounter similar ones in future assessments. The implicit study outcome they aimed to achieve was: "To apply their knowledge and cognitive skills to solve problems similar to those encountered previously on assessments."

These students unknowingly pursued this outcome. They were unaware that their more successful peers were engaging in qualitatively different metacognitive experiences in the same class. Similarly, the successful students did not realize they were having distinctly different learning experiences.

Through my observations of the different interaction patterns among students, I came to understand that both types of students were achieving study outcomes aligned with their respective conceptions of learning. However, since the successful students' conceptions aligned with those of their professors, their study outcomes matched the learning outcomes that were ultimately assessed.

The following comparison allows us to examine the outcomes side by side:

Unsuccessful Students	*Successful Students*
Students must be able to use their knowledge and cognitive skills to solve problems similar to those they had already encountered at a later date on assessments.	Students must be able to use their knowledge and cognitive skills to solve problems they cannot predict in contexts they do not know in advance.

To address this issue, I trained the professor to operate as a choice architect and implement a strategic nudge to encourage students to approach their work from a different perspective. During my observations, I noticed that math faculty would typically go through approximately three problems per class after a brief introduction of the concept. Most of the cognitive heavy lifting was done by the professors and a handful of student thought leaders, while most students passively "learned" by relying on the efforts of these individuals. Instead of actively engaging in their own cognitive work, they relied on vicarious learning through the professors and thought leaders in the classroom. Figure 2.3 illustrates these observations.

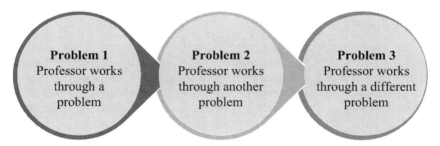

FIGURE 2.3 The former math problem solving structure.

My solution was that the professor restructure the 50-minute class time into five segments of approximately ten minutes each. In the first segment, the professor would introduce the concept, providing a solid foundation for understanding. The subsequent three ten-minute segments would be

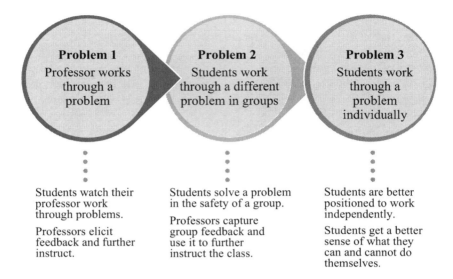

FIGURE 2.4   3×10 math problem solving structure.

dedicated to strategically guiding the class through qualitatively different interactions with the material. This approach would ensure that students actively participate and engage with the content in different ways, promoting deeper learning and understanding. Figure 2.4 illustrates this difference.

This new structure introduced a transformed workspace for students. It began within the classroom, where the professor initially solved problems on the board, following the familiar approach that students were accustomed to. However, during the second problem, a shift occurred as students were organized into groups, allowing them to test their hypotheses in a supportive environment while also learning from their peers' perspectives. Meanwhile, the professor moved around the room, gathering valuable insights into how students interacted with the material.

In the third problem, a critical segment, students were given the opportunity to work independently. This was an important shift because it allowed them to experience working through a problem on their own, right in the class setting. Previously, students had mistakenly believed they could handle tasks outside of class that they were actually unprepared for, leading to feelings of frustration and disappointment. By bringing this experience into the classroom, it became a formative self-assessment, a reality check, for students.

Lastly, in the final ten-minute segment of class, the professor provided the familiar support of clarification, feedback, and guidance, which students had come to expect from their high school experience. This comprehensive approach received high praise from both professors and students. Teachers immediately noticed improved interactions and exchanges between themselves and students, as well as among the students themselves. They also observed a decrease in the number of students requiring reteaching or additional review sessions, while students demonstrated better preparedness for class. Their experiences aligned with students' reports of increased confidence that what they were learning would align with what would be assessed in their tests.

Workspace in Action Example #2

Mrs. Hines, an experienced instructor at a two-year college in western Illinois, had long been grappling with three recurring complaints from her students: (1) covering an excessive amount of material, (2) encountering irrelevant content, and (3) being assigned an overwhelming amount of reading. She made various attempts to address these concerns, such as incorporating tutors into her classes, providing one-on-one sessions, and even allowing students to read during class time (a departure from the norm). However, none of these methods yielded significant improvements in student performance.

I had the opportunity to meet Mrs. Hines during a conference at Appalachian State University in Boone, North Carolina, where I was a speaker. As part of a month-long residential summer institute assignment, she decided to implement the three steps mentioned earlier. Table 2.1 illustrates the

TABLE 2.1 Comparison of Mrs. Hines's Old Versus Metacognitive Learning Outcomes

Old Learning Outcomes	Metacognitive Learning Outcomes
Appreciate the nature and form of literature.	Explain the nature and form of literature in essay form on exams.
Describe literatures of various cultures around the world.	Identify distinct content and cultural features of literature from different areas of the world and express your knowledge in writing assignments.
Demonstrate an internationalist perspective in writing.	Explain an internationalist perspective to world literature in writing assignments.
Analyze key elements of major literary genres.	Distinguish the characteristics of the major literary genres—poetry, essays, fiction, drama, myth, and folklore, and express your knowledge on essay exams.
	Write critical analyses of literature based on analysis of elements of fiction and/or drama.

comparison between Mrs. Hines's previous learning outcomes and the metacognitive learning outcomes (MLOs) she introduced.

These practices introduced by Mrs. Hines helped her students initiate the process of self-regulating their learning. In high school, teachers took on the responsibility of planning, monitoring, and evaluating students' learning. A crucial aspect of this regulation was contextualizing the course, mapping the relationships between the content taught and the desired outcomes. As a college instructor, Mrs. Hines believed it was not her role to perform this mental work for her students. However, her students unconsciously sought this guidance. As a compromise, she developed MLOs and shared their value with her students. The MLOs served as navigational tools, enabling students to establish clear learning targets and monitor their progress towards them, as described by (O'Brien & Cohen, 2008).

Once the students began using the MLOs, the next step was to create a workspace tailored for college. They chose to utilize one of the college's study rooms in the learning center, attracted by the whiteboards and comfortable seating it offered. However, the true value of the workspace became evident in how the students utilized it. They took on many of the tasks that their high school teacher had previously performed and that Mrs. Hines had refrained from doing. For instance, they diligently recorded each important concept covered by Mrs. Hines, consulting the textbook and online resources to gain further clarity. They reviewed their class notes, specifically seeking coherence across the material. Finally, they assessed their level of knowledge against the course outcomes, generating profound questions that they could pose to Mrs. Hines during subsequent classes.

Mrs. Hines was immensely impressed by the students' level of inquiry, firmly believing that they would excel. Her conviction proved correct, as this class achieved the highest overall grade she had ever witnessed, with a significant improvement in the class mean score.

Creating a workspace conducive to college not only enhanced overall class performance but also made teaching more gratifying for Mrs. Hines. This reciprocal benefit is a common outcome when students are rescued from transition traps. Nonetheless, the work does not end there; students must also learn how to labor effectively in their workspaces. This will be the focus of the next chapter.

3

DIVISION OF LABOR TRAP

A recurring issue that I frequently encounter in my interactions with educators and students revolves around the question of how to help students make meaningful contributions to their academic work. Teachers exert considerable effort inside and outside the classroom to educate and develop their students, while students dedicate themselves to learning the material diligently. Despite their shared commitment, there are instances where students fail to meet expectations and perform below par. In the aftermath of such situations, it becomes tempting for teachers and students to blame each other for the unsatisfactory outcomes. However, I have discovered that neither party is entirely to blame. The true culprit lies in their lack of awareness regarding the specific types of labor required to produce the desired work products. As a result, they toil harder in their respective ways, but their efforts do not yield the expected results. Unfortunately, the harder they work, the deeper they fall into the division of labor trap.

In this chapter, we explore the detrimental effects of poorly divided labor on both instructors and students, and explore the liberating sense of freedom experienced by teachers when labor is appropriately divided. I begin by differentiating between academic work and labor. Through vivid examples of teachers and students caught in division of labor traps, I present a framework of choice architecture that can help students make more effective contributions to the teaching and learning process. We conclude the chapter by examining how some of our colleagues have utilized my metacognitive learning outcomes rubric to empower students to produce higher-quality work. Additionally, we share inspiring reflections from students and

DOI: 10.4324/9781003447252-4

educators on the transformative effects of operating in an environment free from division of labor traps.

Distinguishing Academic Work from Labor

Work and *labor* share many similarities, but they are not the same. When I employ the term "labor," I'm referring to a concept that is deeper, more abstract, and qualitatively different than "work." In his book, *The Gift: Creativity and the Artist in the Modern World*, Lewis Hyde distinguishes between the two:

> Work is what we do by the hour. It begins and ends at a specific time and, if possible, we do it for money. Welding car bodies on an assembly line is work; washing dishes, computing taxes, walking the rounds in a psychiatric ward, picking asparagus—these are work. Labor, on the other hand, sets its own pace. We may get paid for it, but it's harder to quantify. ... Writing a poem, raising a child, developing a new calculus, resolving a neurosis, invention in all forms—these are labors.
>
> *(2007, p. 63)*

In the academic context, work refers to quantifiable aspects such as the number of instructional hours taught by teachers or the volume of assignments assigned to students. For students, work entails attending classes, studying, reading, and writing. However, merely engaging in these activities does not guarantee the production of high-quality work products. The key factor lies in the type of labor invested in the work.

Students often confuse work with labor, focusing solely on the amount of time they spend studying, reading, and writing. However, they often overlook the mental labor necessary for producing excellent work products. Tragically, they may work diligently, but without the appropriate labor, their work products fall short. Herein lies the opportunity for us to assist students. By clarifying the labor required, distinguishing between its different types, and dividing it effectively, students can make more meaningful contributions to their academic work. These enhanced contributions not only improve their learning and performance but also alleviate our instructional burden significantly.

The Importance of Dividing Labor in College

When students enter college, they possess proficiency in microlabor. They bring with them a preference for this type of work. However, for students to thrive in college, they must also become proficient in macrolabor. Microlabor entails actions students take to grasp the inputs of academic work, such as attending classes, taking notes, organizing and studying them, and reading course materials. It involves reflecting on the accumulated inputs, ensuring a comprehensive understanding of the information provided. I often explain to students that when they focus on the inputs, they are engaged in microlabor. I refer to this approach as "studying out of the rear-view mirror." However, to truly thrive in college, students must not solely rely on looking backward. They must also learn to engage in macrolabor. Macrolabor comprises actions students take to produce the outcomes of academic work. This type of labor is less quantifiable as it requires abstract thinking. Macrolabor involves achieving conceptual clarity, connecting concepts across different courses, consolidating ideas, and synthesizing knowledge. It is forward-looking work, aimed at using the inputs to generate outcomes.

When students focus on using the inputs to respond to unknown situations, particularly those encountered in assessments, they are engaging in macrolabor. I refer to this approach as "looking ahead through the windshield." Surprisingly, many students fail to engage in macrolabor. They constantly look backward, fixated on the inputs, rather than driving forward toward the outcomes. You may wonder why students don't embrace a forward-looking approach to studying. The reason is that they require us to divide the labor for them. When we divide the labor, students can engage in both microlabor and macrolabor, creating a dual contribution that fosters the acquisition of inputs and the production of outcomes. Before we explore how to divide labor effectively, let us first examine the impact of undivided labor on students and teachers.

The Effects of Undivided Labor on Students

In the absence of a division of labor, students may diligently perform the right tasks but in the wrong manner. For instance, let's consider the case of Ethan, a sophomore student from Lenoir-Rhyne University who participated in my 2013 session on transforming good students into great learners. Ethan recorded a testimonial where he shared his experience. He mentioned that he used to take copious notes and study them before exams. However, after learning about the division of labor, he realized that his notes were only useful for answering specific questions that his professors were unlikely to ask (Projects, 2022). He acknowledged that his notetaking approach had served him well throughout high school but proved inadequate in college. Ethan realized that he needed to employ his notes differently. He recognized the need to change the labor he invested in both taking and studying notes. Prior to the session, Ethan's work primarily involved microlaboring, focusing on mastering the inputs. However, during the session, he learned how to engage in macrolabor and work towards the outcomes. As a result, his notes became more meaningful to him, and his grades improved from Ds to As in multiple courses.

The Impact of Undivided Labor on Teachers

When labor is undivided, teachers may unintentionally incentivize improper behaviors and undermine students' future success. I have witnessed this scenario in my consultations with various institutions, including a recent case at Texas Southmost College, a Hispanic-serving two-year institution in Brownsville, TX. Dr. Mueller shared an elaborate instructional routine she employed with her students. She covered the content and made herself available for additional teaching time when needed. She established various checkpoints where students were expected to share their work progress. Depending on their status, she provided additional support. At first glance, one might commend Dr. Mueller for modeling effective teaching practices. However, Dr. Mueller then revealed that her students performed well in her class but struggled in other courses where instructors did not go to such lengths to ensure their students were studying and preparing adequately. She shared the feedback she received from a recent graduate who excelled in her class but was failing at the four-year university she currently attended. Dr. Mueller believed that this student would continue to thrive. So, why was she struggling? Dr. Mueller realized that she was assuming too much of the labor that students needed to undertake independently. She was overworking herself while underworking her students. By "underworking," I don't mean she didn't require them to do anything. Dr. Mueller had high expectations and assigned a considerable amount of work. However, the students were primarily engaged in microlabor, while she was shouldering the burden of macrolabor. It was only when their contributions were combined that the desired outcomes could be produced. Dr. Mueller's instructional approach generated positive reviews from colleagues at her institution. But it did not help students succeed in courses where they were expected to independently engage in both microlabor and macrolabor.

Division of Labor Schedule

Within the education system, many high school teachers inadvertently encourage students to rely solely on microlabor, neglecting the development of macrolabor skills. As a consequence, when these students enter our courses, they often struggle and default to microlabor practices. However, being aware of this tendency presents us with an opportunity to guide them toward better labor practices.

To address this issue, it is crucial for educators to provide students with a new framework for dividing labor in our courses, programs, and schools. In my approach, I have developed a Division of Labor Framework that is deeply rooted in the Backwards Design Process (BDP) and Choice Architecture theory. To refresh your memory from the introduction, recall that the BDP aids teachers in conceptualizing and organizing instruction well before determining the course content to be covered. It comprises three distinct stages, each serving a specific purpose.

Stage 1: Identifying Desired Results

In the initial stage of the BDP, we focus on identifying the desired results we want our students to achieve. By clearly defining the outcomes we aim for, we lay the foundation for effective instruction and learning. This stage allows us to begin with the end in mind, guiding us in shaping the labor practices of our students.

Stage 2: Designing Assessment Methods

Moving on to the second stage, we determine how and when we will assess our students. By carefully selecting appropriate assessment methods, we ensure that students' progress aligns with the desired results identified in the previous stage. Assessment serves as a crucial feedback mechanism, informing both students and educators about the effectiveness of their labor practices.

Stage 3: Planning Content and Instruction

In the final stage of the BDP, we decide on the specific content to be covered and how we will deliver it. This stage involves designing instructional strategies, materials, and activities that will enable students to achieve the desired results and excel in their assessments. Here, choice architecture theory comes into play, as it emphasizes the importance of how we design our instruction to shape students' labor practices.

I prefer to synthesize these theories as a way of prompting students to adopt a new perspective and practice of macrolabor as the default mode of learning. You can use the following table to this approach to encourage students to regulate their learning automatically and with relative ease. By providing students with a well-structured framework based on the BDP stages, we empower them to develop effective labor practices and succeed in their educational journey. You can use the following steps over a four-week period to encourage students to begin macrolaboring.

Week 1	Step 1	Introduce students to the Academic Work Formula. Encourage them to internalize the formula as a constant reminder that their efforts involve transforming inputs into outcomes.
	Step 2	Teach students how to utilize the tools within your syllabus, rather than treating it as a mere document. Specific sections of the syllabus, such as topics, content areas, and especially Metacognitive Learning Outcomes (MLOs), offer an overview of the inputs and outcomes students must navigate in your course. Students should use this information to apply the academic work formula.
		MLOs serve as destinations that students should strive to reach through their labor and work. Additionally, MLOs guide students by clarifying which inputs correspond to specific outcomes and provide guidance on how to process the inputs effectively. Without understanding and utilizing the MLOs, students may struggle to manage their learning productively, potentially leading to futile labor.
Weeks 2–3	Step 3	Demonstrate the application of the academic work formula using relevant course materials. Separate the content, cognitive aspects, and conceptual elements of your course. Show students the connections between the inputs they engage with and the desired knowledge specified by the learning outcomes. This modeling process enables students to understand the relationships between their efforts and the expected results.
Week 4	Step 4	By this point in the college course, a significant assessment is typically approaching. As enough content has been covered, this becomes an ideal opportunity to guide students in integrating the content, cognitive processes, and conceptual understanding of your course. Show them how to synthesize the inputs and outcomes effectively. It's important to note that full integration may not be possible until we cover the Cognitive Traps section, but you can provide students with a glimpse of what they can and cannot achieve at this stage.

By implementing the division of labor framework and following the four steps outlined above, educators can successfully guide students towards adopting macrolabor practices. This approach not only facilitates more effective learning but also enables teachers to deliver impactful instruction while reducing their workload.

Application of the Division of Labor Framework

Now, let's explore an example from a calculus course that illustrates the practical application of these four steps. We will examine how these steps can be employed in a calculus course to empower students to engage in macrolabor from the very beginning of the semester. By following this example, both students and instructors can experience the benefits of this transformative approach to learning and teaching.

	Step	Application of Step
Week 1 Step 1	Introduce the academic work formula and promote its continuous use as a reminder of converting inputs into outcomes. To reinforce this concept, provide students with large note cards and encourage them to write down course outcomes, placing them somewhere highly visible, such as on their mirror or within the outer plastic cover of their notebook.	The calculus professor should introduce the formula and emphasize the importance of committing it to memory and reviewing it frequently during the first week of school. Some teachers have even suggested having students write it on their mirrors to reinforce the message each morning.
Step 2	Teach students how to utilize the syllabus as a tool rather than a mere document. Highlight specific segments of the syllabus, such as topics, content areas, and Metacognitive Learning Outcomes (MLOs), which provide an overview of the inputs and outcomes students will encounter throughout the course. Emphasize that MLOs serve as destinations for students' labor and indicate which inputs correspond to specific outcomes. Additionally, MLOs provide guidance on how to process the inputs effectively. By pointing out key areas in the syllabus, such as early topics and their importance, students begin to view the syllabus as a valuable tool for managing their learning.	During this step, the calculus professor would highlight important sections of the syllabus that require early focus from students. For instance, the professor would draw students' attention to the topics outlined on page 6 that will be covered in the initial days of the course, as well as the schedule of topics presented on page 7. Furthermore, the professor would emphasize the significance of the first, and possibly the second, learning outcome. Although this step doesn't consume much time, implementing it during the first week serves as a potent regulatory prompt for students. It prompts them to perceive the syllabus not merely as a document but as a valuable tool for guiding their academic work.

(*Continued*)

(Continued)

| Weeks 2–3 | Step 3 | Utilize course material to demonstrate how the academic work formula operates. Separate the content into distinct categories: cognitive, conceptual, and content elements. Show students the relationships between the inputs and outcomes of the course. | For example, the professor can explain calculus concepts like the chain rule and related rates, guiding students to apply these concepts correctly. Provide samples of course content, such as notes or textbook materials, that demonstrate the outcomes (related rates or chain rule) along with the associated learning outcomes. While refraining from explicitly revealing the relationship between inputs and outcomes, assign students a reflective homework assignment to encourage them to contemplate these connections. This approach sets the stage for self-regulated learning. |
| Week 4 | Step 4 | As major assessments approach, students have acquired the necessary information to regulate their learning effectively. At this stage, teachers demonstrate how to integrate the content, cognitive, and conceptual elements of the course. While the complete synthesis may require further exploration, it is now feasible to introduce tools like the ThinkWell-LearnWell Diagram from the Cognitive Traps section. | In this final step, teachers demonstrate how students can use tools, such as the ThinkWell-LearnWell Diagram in conjunction with the MLOs to help students convert their accumulated notes and other course content into the appropriate outcomes. |

By following these steps, students can engage in macrolabor practices within the first month of the course. This approach not only facilitates their learning but also enables instructors to deliver impactful instruction while minimizing their teaching workload.

In conclusion, achieving the right types of labor between educators and students marks an important milestone, but our journey towards effective learning doesn't end there. It is crucial to understand where true learning occurs. In the upcoming chapter, we will complete the structural traps section by moving away from the classroom to explore the Locus of Learning Trap.

Assessment Questions

1 What steps have you taken as a college teacher to clearly communicate the division of labor between yourself and your students in your course?
2 How do you ensure that students understand the desired outcomes and expectations for their labor in your course?
3 Have you observed any instances where students have relied solely on microlabor without engaging in macrolabor? If so, how can you address this issue?
4 What strategies or tools do you use to promote student agency and self-regulation in their learning process?
5 How do you assess whether students are effectively managing their learning and utilizing the division of labor framework to their advantage?

Assessment Questions for Students

1 Describe the specific tasks or activities you have been focusing on in your recent coursework. How do these tasks contribute to your overall learning goals for the course?
2 Can you explain the broader purpose or objective behind the work you have been doing in your assignments? How does it relate to the larger concepts or skills you are expected to develop?
3 Reflect on your study habits and preparation for exams. Do you primarily focus on memorizing individual facts and details, or do you engage in deeper understanding and synthesis of concepts?
4 How do you approach the organization and planning of your coursework? Do you break it down into smaller, manageable tasks, or do you consider the larger picture and connect different components to achieve your learning objectives?
5 Consider your learning experiences outside of class, such as participating in discussions, engaging in study groups, or reading scholastic resources. How do these activities contribute to your overall learning and growth as a student?

These questions can help students reflect on their learning approach and distinguish whether they are primarily engaged in microlabor (task-oriented, focusing on isolated activities) or macrolabor (strategic, connecting tasks to broader goals and understanding). By encouraging your students to critically evaluate their own learning practices, you can support them in developing a more holistic and effective approach to their education.

Exercises for Students

1 Reflective Journaling: Ask students to maintain a journal throughout the course where they can regularly reflect on their learning process, identify instances where they may have fallen into division of labor traps, and propose strategies to overcome them.
2 Group Discussions: Divide students into small groups and assign them specific topics or concepts from the course. Encourage them to discuss and collaboratively identify the division of labor required to understand and master those topics effectively.
3 Self-Assessment Worksheets: Use the Academic Labor checklist (You can obtain the appendix and additional supporting materials at the following online location: http://www.routledge.com/9781642672893) to help students assess their microlabor and macrolabor practices.

Class Activity

Role-Playing Scenarios: In this exercise, students will step into the role of teachers and engage in hypothetical scenarios to practice applying the Division of Labor Framework. Their task is to distinguish between microlabor practices and macrolabor practices, and then develop an effective study sequence. Here's a clearer version of the exercise:

1 Scenario Creation: Assign students specific segments of material to work with, such as a chapter or a topic from the course curriculum. Ask them to create hypothetical scenarios where they take on the role of the teacher for that particular segment.
2 Division of Labor Framework: Students should apply the Division of Labor Framework to their scenarios. They need to identify and separate microlabor practices (smaller tasks) from macrolabor practices (bigger-picture activities). For example, microlabor might involve reading specific sections, watching tutorial videos, or solving practice problems, while macrolabor could involve summarizing key concepts, matching discreet content with respective learning outcomes, or identifying gaps between daily content and learning outcomes.
3 Study Sequence Development: Once students have distinguished between micro- and macrolabor practices, they should develop a proper

study sequence for themselves or hypothetical students. This sequence should outline the order in which the activities should be completed to facilitate effective learning, which ultimately entails producing the course outcomes. Emphasize the importance of considering the logical progression of concepts and ensuring that macrolabor activities support the achievement of the desired learning outcomes.

By engaging in this role-playing exercise, students will gain a deeper understanding of the Division of Labor Framework and its application to effective studying. They will learn to distinguish between micro- and macrolabor practices, and develop a well-structured study sequence that optimizes their learning experience.

4
LOCUS OF LEARNING TRAP

At the University of California at San Diego, I met Stacey, whose journey serves as a compelling illustration of the Locus of Learning Trap. In high school, her days were packed from 7:15 am to 2:15 pm with classes, followed by extracurricular activities until 5:00 or 6:00 pm, depending on the season. Any unfinished homework had to be squeezed into the evenings after dinner and chores at home.

When Stacey entered college, she clung to her old habits. Despite the stark differences in her college class and practice schedules, she persisted in waiting until after dinner to study and work on assignments. Throughout the day, she spent her free time socializing, catching up on sleep, or scrolling through social media, while her evening hours were spent hanging out and exploring her new college social scenes. Unfortunately, her grades suffered until I taught her how to maximize the daylight hours.

Stacey reflects on her experience, stating, "When I learned to maximize my daylight hours, I immediately saw a difference. It was like the time was always there, but I wasted it on trivial things."

To help our students become independent learners, we must shift their perspective on time management and align it with the college schedule. The conveyer-belt model prevalent in high school involves completing most of the work during class time, leaving evenings and nights for studying or review. This approach made sense in high school, where time was scarce due to continuous classes and extracurricular activities. However, it proves ineffective in the bustling college environment.

Think of time as a suitcase: the space you have depends on how you pack things.

DOI: 10.4324/9781003447252-5

Successful and unsuccessful students adopt contrasting approaches to time utilization. Successful students excel at maximizing the college schedule by strategically exploiting daylight hours. This time-management skill becomes crucial, especially for students living on campus. They recognize that college operates on a gapped class model, providing numerous opportunities for academic work while the sun is still shining.

Stacey's journey serves as a powerful lesson. She realized that studying at night worked in high school primarily because it was often the only available time due to the continuous class model. However, she discovered that college offers more flexibility, with gaps in the schedule that can be utilized for productive academic work. By effectively managing her daylight hours, Stacey harnessed these openings to ensure she had sufficient time for both work and play.

This chapter presents the Locus of Learning Trap and explores strategies and techniques to maximize the daylight hours. By empowering our students to recognize the potential within their college schedules, we can help them make the most of their time, achieve academic success, and still savor a fulfilling college experience.

The Structural Gap Delusion

You may have noticed a common pattern among college students: their intentions to study often exceed their actual study time. To explore this further, I conducted a simple study with students, asking them to estimate their study hours for the week on Sundays, and then comparing it with their actual study time the following Sunday. The results were striking. Most students overestimated their study time, ultimately studying far less than they had predicted. When questioned about this discrepancy, their responses usually revolved around time slipping away or unforeseen distractions taking precedence. In essence, they admitted to mismanaging their time.

While many educators witness students struggling with time management, they often underestimate the challenges faced by new college students. Those who overestimated their study hours genuinely believed their estimates were accurate at the time. They were not deliberately lying or misleading; they were ensnared in a delusion that led them to believe they would spend their time as planned, even though the reality proved otherwise. This phenomenon is what I refer to as the structural gap delusion.

The transition to college can be particularly challenging for students in terms of managing their time effectively. When students discover gaps in their class schedules, they tend to fill those spaces with activities like napping, gaming, streaming shows, or socializing, assuming they will compensate by studying at night. However, the allure of the college nightlife often proves too tempting, and studying never truly materializes. This process unfolds in a somewhat deceptive manner. Let me share an example of how the structural gap delusion played out for Kareem, Vickie's son from the Structural Traps section.

Soon after I began working with Kareem, I quickly suspected that he had fallen victim to the structural gap delusion. As Kareem recounted his daily routine, it became clear that he filled his schedule gaps with naps, television, and socializing. He would then attempt to study in the evenings, but distractions would derail his efforts. Here is a glimpse into his experience.

On a Monday, after attending the Clemson football game, Kareem attended classes and met with his academic coach. He planned to study in the evening since he had scheduled naps and socializing during the day. After dinner and spending time with friends, Kareem sat down in his room around 7:00 pm to study. However, just as he settled into his studies, he received a text from his friends, inviting him to meet some girls at a local spot. At this juncture, Kareem faced a choice: prioritize studying or join his friends. As it was early in the week, he convinced himself that he could indulge in the outing and still have time to complete his work later.

Here, Kareem entered the first phase of delusion, assuring himself that he would study upon returning from the evening adventure. Importantly, this was not a deliberate lie; Kareem genuinely intended to study later that evening. However, when he returned home, fatigue set in. Despite seeing his books and notebook open on his desk, illuminated by the lamp, he reasoned that he would leave the light on and wake up early in the morning before classes to study. Again, Kareem would pass a lie detector test because his intention to study was genuine. He even set his alarm for 5:00 am, providing ample time for work before his 8:00 am class on Tuesday. He had now entered a new phase of delusion.

When Tuesday morning arrived, Kareem found himself still exhausted. The previous night, he had not anticipated how tired he would be. He repeatedly hit the snooze button on his alarm until he realized it was already 7:40 am, leaving him with little time to rush off to class.

Hope arose with the start of a new day, as Kareem aspired to reset his schedule and get back on track. Unfortunately, the same cycle of delusion persisted. After his classes ended at 4:00 pm, Kareem, still fatigued from the previous night, grabbed a quick meal and returned to his room to study. However, after a mere 15 minutes of studying, exhaustion overcame him, and he fell asleep, only to be awakened by a text from a girl he had met the night before. Engrossed in their conversation, he soon grew tired and called it a night. Yet, before turning off the desk lamp, he convinced himself that he would study in the morning.

This pattern repeated intermittently over the next few weeks, with Kareem managing only a few sporadic hours of studying. As Monday's test approached, he realized the gravity of the situation. He also recognized that Clemson was playing one of the biggest football games of the year on Saturday. Kareem made a plan to hang out on Friday, study early on Saturday before the game, attend the game, and dedicate the entire day on Sunday to studying.

During the weekend, Kareem managed to squeeze in some study time, but he soon realized that it was insufficient to adequately prepare himself. He did the best he could and showed up for Monday's tests, hoping he had done enough while also acknowledging the possibility of being ill-prepared.

Some may view Kareem's predicament as a mere time management issue. They may try to impose a schedule on him. But this remedy would have a short lifecycle. Kareem was trapped in the structural gap delusion, still perceiving the college schedule as a continuation of the structured high school model. Having grown accustomed to studying primarily in the evening hours, he failed to grasp that this approach is not conducive to success in college.

Rescue Strategy

To help students like Kareem, the first step is to shift their perspective from a continuous schedule mindset to a gapped schedule framework. I emphasized to Kareem that excelling academically in college required him to make the most of the daylight hours. Anticipating his objections about his busy life, I shared stories of other students who faced greater commitments yet still managed to complete their work while maintaining an active social life. The key was their ability to utilize the gaps in their schedule for studying, which then granted them the freedom to enjoy social activities without guilt or unfinished work hanging over their heads.

In addressing this issue, it is crucial to acknowledge that the battle for students' study time is fierce. Multi-million- and billion-dollar industries, such as social media platforms, the video game industry, television streaming, and sports networks, compete for students' attention and time. These industries have invested significant resources in occupying students' minds, making them formidable rivals in the marketplace of students' attention.

For many students, it is essential for them to see that there is room for their social life before they can commit to a study schedule. That's why I always begin the schedule-making process by asking students to select two days that they want to keep free for fun and social activities. These designated "fun days" help alleviate their fears of being confined to a rigid schedule. Addressing this concern upfront is crucial and serves as a necessary starting point for many students.

Once we have addressed their need for fun, we can proceed to the next step, which involves helping students identify two hours each day dedicated to studying. These two hours can be consecutive or separate, but they should consist of at least one-hour timeframes. Collaboratively, we create their schedule, visually illustrating what it would look like. I have conducted this exercise with students nationwide, and each time, they are astounded by how appealing the schedule appears to them. They are surprised to discover how much available time they have for academic work.

When I initially started working with Kareem, he firmly believed that fitting in ten hours of study time per week was an impossible feat given his busy lifestyle. However, once I showed him how to maximize the daylight hours effectively, he realized that he had ample time for studying and still enough room for social activities. Kareem and I then created a schedule that optimally managed the daylight hours, as exemplified in Figure 4.1.

As you observe Kareem's schedule, you'll notice that he has designated Friday and Saturday as his "no study days." When Kareem marked those days first, I could sense his resistance diminishing as he realized he would have time for the social activities he cherished. These activities were an important aspect of why he chose Clemson as his college home. It's common for teachers to downplay students' desire for fun and solely emphasize their role as students. While it's true that academics are the foremost part of college life, we must acknowledge that college encompasses more than just classes for students. It becomes their home and community. Just as we consider various factors like community amenities, schools, and natural resources when selecting our place of residence based, students also have multiple reasons for choosing a college. While obtaining a degree is their primary goal, it is not their only reason. Addressing their desire for fun and enjoyment greatly facilitates the scheduling process.

Moving forward, Kareem's schedule demonstrates a mix of one-hour and two-hour time slots throughout the week. These hours are based on his class schedule, sleep preferences, extracurricular activities, and any other interests that he knows will compete for his time and attention. At this point, I haven't asked Kareem to stop any current activities. I have simply shown him that there is enough time within his existing lifestyle to accommodate a ten-hour study schedule. Kareem was pleasantly surprised by the availability of time in his schedule. Initially, he believed his days were already fully occupied. However, now he realizes that he has ample daytime hours to dedicate to his studies.

Another noteworthy aspect of Kareem's schedule is that his evenings are entirely open. Apart from his computer applications class from 6:00 pm to 8:30 pm on Mondays and his work-study job from 7:30 pm to 9:30 pm on Tuesdays, Kareem finishes his commitments by 6:00 pm. This arrangement works effectively for him. From an empathetic standpoint, for a strategy to be successful, it must appeal to the person implementing it. In the past, I

Time	Monday	Tuesday	Wednesday	Thursday	Friday	Saturday	Sunday
						no study day	*no study day*
8.00-8.50 a.m.	Freshman Seminar	Calculus		Calculus			
9.00-9.50 a.m.		Study Time			Meet with Academic Coach		
10.00-10.50 a.m.				Study Time			Study Time
11.00-11.50 a.m.	Chemistry		Chemistry		Chemistry		
12.00-12.50 p.m.	Micro Econ.		Micro Econ.		Micro Econ.		
1.00-1.50 p.m.	Psych.	Study Time	Psych.		Psych.		
2.00-2.50 p.m.	Study Time						
3.00-3.50 p.m.				Work Study			
4.00-4.50 p.m.		Work Study	Study Time				
5.00-5.50 p.m.							
6.00-6.50 p.m.	Computer Applications						
7.00-7.50 p.m.							
8.00-8.50 p.m.		Work Study					
9.00-9.50 p.m.							

FIGURE 4.1   Managing the daylight hours (sample schedule).

used to create schedules with students based on my preferences, and they would leave with a fully detailed schedule. I felt satisfied after those sessions, but I realized that students weren't adhering to the schedules. However, by prioritizing fun and involving students in the schedule-making process as allies, they become more invested in and committed to the schedule. In fact, many students report surpassing the initially allotted ten-hour study time.

Concluding the schedule-making process with students, I always caution them against the temptation to believe that having a schedule or merely following it will magically solve their problems. Instead of solely emphasizing the schedule, I inform them that it serves as a structure that provides them with time to adapt to the college environment, which presents unfamiliar gaps and nightly temptations. Creating a schedule to maximize the daylight hours prevents them from falling into the illusion of unstructured time. However, the real magic lies in how they utilize and dedicate themselves during their scheduled study hours. The structure merely offers them an opportunity to become successful independent learners.

SECTION II
Functional Traps

One morning, while on my way to the office, I ran across Bryce, a sophomore student who studied so much in the library that one may assume that he lived there. Bryce was the epitome of a diligent student. He stood out amongst his peers since his freshman year. He held leadership positions in the Student Government Association and two other organizations, dressed impeccably, and displayed a genuine commitment to academics. Every time I saw Bryce, he was either engrossed in reading or tucked away in a corner, taking meticulous notes with highlighters, pens, and even a three-ring hole-puncher. It was evident that Bryce took his studies seriously.

However, one particular interaction with Bryce caught me off guard. As I passed him that morning, I asked about his classes, expecting a brief response of "great!" But to my surprise, Bryce's eyes filled with concern as he replied, "Not well!" Intrigued, I inquired further, expecting him to share a story of disappointment over receiving his first-ever B grade on an exam. Instead, Bryce confessed, "I haven't passed a single test in my biology course yet." It was a baffling revelation. How could a diligent and intelligent student like Bryce be struggling so much? Intrigued by his situation, I invited Bryce to my office to delve deeper into the matter.

Curious to understand the root of Bryce's struggles, I asked him to describe his professor. He reflexively responded, "She sucks!" This harsh

DOI: 10.4324/9781003447252-6

criticism seemed entirely out of character for Bryce, prompting me to seek elaboration. He explained,

> My professor is terrible! I feel like I'm wasting my money. She covers all this material in class, but none of it is ever on her tests. I'll do the work; she just needs to tell me what I need to know!

In those five sentences, Bryce encapsulated the essence of what I refer to as a functional trap.

Functional Traps Introduction

Functional traps emerge from the disparity between the instructional approaches students are accustomed to in high school and college, as well as the differing roles that educators play in these environments. In high school, students not only learn "what to learn" through the established curriculum but also absorb the implicit lessons of "how to learn." While colleges and universities assume that students with a strong curricular foundation will excel in the college environment, this assumption doesn't always hold true.

Bryce's previous academic achievements in high school did not equip him to thrive in his biology course. His inability to translate his efforts into good grades left him feeling like he was wasting his money and his professor was ineffective. Bryce was accustomed to teachers explicitly directing his learning, and he diligently followed their guidance. However, when his college professor evaluated him on material not explicitly covered in class, Bryce found himself utterly lost.

Bryce's story serves as a cautionary tale, one that highlights a common trap in higher education. It is a trap that can derail even the most diligent and determined students, a trap I have encountered before and recognized the severe consequences it can have. As I conversed with Bryce that day, I realized his experience was not unique. Similar narratives were unfolding on campuses across the country, demanding attention and intervention. This was a story that needed to be shared, empowering other students to avoid falling into the same trap.

Coincidentally, I received a distressing call from a parent whose daughter, Shayla, attended Vanderbilt University, fearing that she was on the verge of losing her academic scholarship. Shayla, an honors student from a renowned private high school, excelled in extracurricular activities. Yet, as a freshman at Vanderbilt, she struggled immensely. Her mother wrote,

> She is constantly frustrated, no matter how much she studies, which seems to be all the time nowadays. This is a new and surprising experience

for us since she excelled in these courses previously. Shayla questions her tools and abilities to succeed in such an academically rigorous environment. She's heartbroken, and I believe you hold the key to helping Shayla regain her lost confidence.

Both Lenoir-Rhyne University and Vanderbilt University implemented entrance criteria to ensure that students like Bryce and Shayla possessed the necessary background and knowledge for college success. However, the assumption that a robust high school curriculum automatically translates to success in college is flawed. This assumption leads to a series of misguided beliefs, including the notion that working hard and being rewarded for one's efforts, the American dream, will naturally materialize in the college setting. Furthermore, it presumes that students who struggle lack resilience or possess the wrong mindset. By adhering to these assumptions, we unknowingly apply the Papa John's perspective to students: "Give me better students, and I'll give you better results." This mindset overlooks the complex factors influencing student success and undermines our ability to help all students reach their full potential.

The stories of Bryce and Shayla resonate deeply within the landscape of higher education, challenging the assumptions many of us hold about the transition from high school to college. Since I published an article titled "Why Good Students do 'Bad' in College" on my website in 2013, I have received numerous accounts from parents and students who have undergone similar experiences. I have engaged with parents of incoming college students who hold hope that their child's prior high school achievements will adequately prepare them for the challenges of college. However, as demonstrated by Bryce and Shayla's cases, many students encounter significant difficulties despite their impressive high school track records. Hence, it is imperative that we reevaluate our assumptions regarding college readiness and the multifaceted factors that contribute to student success in higher education.

How Functional Traps Affect Students

Students such as Bryce and Shayla find themselves in functional traps not because they are unwilling or unable to put in the necessary work to learn the established curriculum, but because they struggle to navigate the hidden curriculum. The hidden curriculum encompasses the implicit elements of a course that students must decipher to understand their roles in the teaching and learning process. Unfortunately, these cues are often missing or misunderstood, leaving students without the necessary guidance to succeed in the academic environment.

The functional traps that students encounter can be likened to being caught between a "rock" and a "hard place." The rock represents the visible and tangible challenges of the established curriculum, which students can study, plan for, and overcome with the right tools and tactics. In contrast, the hard place represents the hidden curriculum, which is invisible and difficult to navigate. Students may not even realize they are succumbing to its influence until it's too late. Conquering this invisible foe becomes a formidable task for students as they struggle to understand and adapt to its implicit expectations.

The hard place of the hidden curriculum poses a significant challenge for both students and educators due to its two primary characteristics. First, it is invisible, meaning that its impact is often felt but not consciously recognized until it has already affected student performance. Second, those who have successfully navigated the hidden curriculum often do so unconsciously, accepting its norms as the status quo. This creates a disadvantage for students who are not aware of its existence or how to navigate it effectively.

When students underperform in college, the assumption is often that they are unable to overcome the challenges of the established curriculum. As a result, educators may modify their content, instruction, or teaching modalities to address what they perceive as the problem. However, these solutions are ineffective against the hidden curriculum and only serve to frustrate students further. The functional trap holds them back from reaching their potential, leaving them feeling trapped and unable to pinpoint the root of their difficulties.

Bryce's experience is a prime example of a student caught in a functional trap. He was confident in his ability to overcome the visible challenges of the established curriculum, but he struggled when his professor operated outside the role he was accustomed to. Bryce attributed his difficulties to his professor's perceived incompetence, not realizing that he was grappling with the hidden curriculum and unsure of how to function in the teaching and learning relationship.

How Functional Traps Affect Educators

Functional traps not only affect students but also impact educators. As highlighted by Paul Ramsden in his book *Learning to Teach in Higher Education*, he urges educators, "to become a good teacher, first understand your students' experiences of learning" (Ramsden, 2005). Ramsden's choice of words resonates with me, as he emphasizes the importance of going beyond a mere understanding of the content students have encountered prior to college. Instead, he urges us to delve into the context in which students have learned the material, including the roles played by their precollege educators.

Educators who lack this foreknowledge are at risk of misinterpreting certain behaviors, such as students' passive learning approach or their request for a review of previously covered material, as signs of academic unpreparedness. In reality, these responses may stem from the hidden curriculum they have internalized throughout their precollege years.

The High School Teacher's Role vs. The College Teacher's Role

In high school, educators assume the role of task managers, responsible for breaking down academic content and ensuring students grasp the key messages. They provide explicit guidance, reinforce information in various ways, and utilize specific projects and assignments to reinforce learning. Students take on the role of task performers, following the guidance of their teachers and excelling within the established structure. This dynamic shapes students' expectations and roles as they enter college.

On the other hand, college educators, traditionally referred to as professors, have a different approach. The term "professor" stems from a religious context, meaning to declare or profess expertise. College educators expect students to independently navigate and distill complex topics, which requires students to take on roles they may not have experienced or been trained for. This shift in roles and expectations can leave students like Bryce and Shayla caught in functional traps, grappling with the unfamiliar territory of the hidden curriculum.

Bryce and Shayla found themselves ensnared in functional traps, but their interpretations of their experiences diverged significantly. Bryce's frustration was directed outward, squarely aimed at his professor. He believed that she was not fulfilling her role properly and that she was the root cause of the problem. On the other hand, Shayla internalized her predicament and began questioning herself: "Am I capable enough for Vanderbilt?" Additionally, she pondered the preparedness provided by her elite Academy, asking herself, "Did they adequately prepare me for college?"

Functional traps create a dichotomous scenario for students, forcing them into binary choices. They are inclined to believe that either the educator is ineffective or they themselves lack the necessary abilities. It becomes a matter of being right or wrong, with the power dynamics of a course often leading many students to conclude that the professor must be right, therefore they, as students, must be wrong. Whichever way students interpret their experiences within these functional traps, it is detrimental for both students and educators alike.

Functional traps have far-reaching effects, impacting both students and educators. They contribute to negative perceptions students form about their professors and can lead to a negative view of college students among educators. By understanding the nature of functional traps, educators can work towards breaking the cycle of blame and develop strategies to support students in navigating the hidden curriculum.

How do you know whether you've encountered functional traps? Do your students seem disengaged? If so, then they may be ensnared in a functional trap. Do they expect you to provide them a study guide before each test? This too may be an indication of a functional trap. Furthermore, if you or your colleagues actively avoid teaching first-year students altogether, it is possible that you all have fallen into the grasp of functional traps. Recognizing these telltale signs enables educators to identify and address the underlying causes of functional traps, empowering them to cultivate supportive learning environments where students can truly thrive.

In this section we will explore two interconnected functional traps that significantly impact the dynamics between college teachers and students. The first trap is known as the 80/20 Trap, which arises when students' incompatible views of learning, inherited from their high school experiences, clash with the realities of college learning. We will examine how these conflicting perspectives hinder students' academic progress. The second trap, referred to as the pedagogical belief trap, stems from students adopting incorrect beliefs about effective instruction. We will uncover the consequences of these misguided beliefs and their impact on students' learning outcomes. Together, these two traps form the primary drivers of the dysfunctional relationships often observed in college settings. However, this section concludes with a positive outlook, as we explore strategies that teachers can employ to help students develop a fresh vision for academic work and foster a mutually beneficial relationship with their instructors.

Regrettably, functional traps have become so widespread that they are often perceived as a normal part of the educational landscape by many educators. However, if you have encountered the following statements within your institution, it is a clear indication that functional traps are present within your environment:

- "Attending class is a waste of time." (student)
- "My teacher's teaching style doesn't align with my learning style." (student)
- "My students are consistently disrespectful towards me." (faculty)
- "Both teachers and students appear unhappy and dissatisfied with each other." (administrator)

These statements reflect the prevalence of functional traps and highlight the need to address and mitigate their impact on the teaching and learning experience.

5

THE 80/20 PARADIGM TRAP

Imagine two brothers who share the same biological father. The eldest brother believes he must work hard to earn his father's approval and love. He toils endlessly and obediently in the hopes that he will someday earn his father's approval. However, the harder he works, the more he resents his father and his younger brother. On the other hand, the younger brother sees himself as secure with his father and therefore believes he has nothing to prove or earn from his father. He is energized by his labor and generous towards his older brother and others. Though the brothers share the same circumstances, their differing perspectives profoundly influence their interactions with themselves and with others. This parable illustrates how individual beliefs and viewpoints can shape our actions and how we engage with those around us. It serves as a poignant metaphor for understanding how these same factors impact the dynamic between teachers and students.

In academic settings, to truly help students overcome the academic challenges that stem from functional traps, we must understand students' beliefs and perspectives about academic work. Our understanding begins with understanding students' epistemological views, which refer to their views about how they come to know and justify knowledge (Hofer & Pintrich, 2002). These views influence how they approach their academic work and the beliefs that guide their practices.

When you peel back the layers of observable practices students employ to learn material (such as studying their notes, working through problem sets, creating flash cards, or organizing or highlighting their notes) *and* peel back the beliefs that guide those practices (such as their beliefs about how long or

DOI: 10.4324/9781003447252-7

how hard one must study), then you get to students' epistemological views or, in other words, their views about knowing.

Epistemology is a field of philosophy that explores how we come to know and justify knowledge (Hofer & Pintrich, 2002). It explores the question, *how do we come to know what we ultimately know?* As students navigate academic content, they are perpetually guided by their personal epistemic view of the academic world. As Hofer and Pintrich note,

> In the classroom, students regularly encounter new information and may approach the learning process quite differently depending on whether they view knowledge as a set of accumulated facts or an integrated set of constructs, or whether they view themselves as passive receptors or active constructors of knowledge.
>
> *(Hofer & Pintrich, 2002, Location No. 168)*

Understanding students' epistemological or epistemic views is key to unraveling the interactions between how they view themselves (i.e., as passive receptors or active constructors) and how they view knowledge (i.e., as isolated facts or connected constructs). Students' epistemic views frame the following critical questions they continually navigate as they do academic work:

- What is knowledge?
- Is knowledge obtained or developed?
- How is knowledge obtained or developed?
- Who is responsible for obtaining or developing knowledge?
- When, where, and under what conditions is knowledge obtained or developed?

While students may never explicitly ask these questions, they govern every aspect of how they do academic work and their interactions with educators.

As educators, it is essential to understand that every student has an epistemic view, which governs every aspect of their learning and performance. Although it may seem impossible to determine each student's epistemic view, researchers have identified two broad categories under the construct of "approaches to learning" (Entwistle N., 1991, Entwistle N. J., 2001). These categories include a surface approach and a deep approach. Students with a surface approach view academic work as a collection of isolated facts and view themselves as passive receptors of this information. In contrast, students with a deep approach view academic work as an interconnected system of ideas, and they view themselves as active constructors of knowledge (Entwistle N., 1991, Marton, 1976).

Having a clear understanding of students' approach or epistemic viewpoint is crucial because it shapes their "vision" or perception of academic environments. This "vision" ultimately determines what they consider important within academic settings. By comprehending how students view their academic world, we can better tailor our teaching methods and curriculum to align with students' perspectives. In turn, this can lead to increased engagement and motivation for students, as they feel that their needs and perspectives are being acknowledged and addressed. Therefore, it is essential to acknowledge and understand the role that students' "vision" plays in their academic success.

Shifting students from a surface to a deep vision of academic work is difficult because students don't realize that they are seeing the academic world through a particular viewpoint. To them, the way they perceive learning is just how learning works. This can be particularly problematic in college, where the learner-centric model clashes with the teacher-centric approach that often dominates high school education. While students may have been able to get by with a surface approach in high school, college professors expect a deeper level of engagement with the material. Students who don't adjust their approach may find themselves struggling in college.

Overall, the difference between a surface and deep approach to academic work is a crucial distinction between high school and college. Students who recognize the need to put on "scuba gear" and dive more deeply into the material are more likely to succeed in college. However, for those who remain in the shallow waters, the 80/20 trap awaits.

The 80/20 Trap

I frequently ask students the following question: *In high school, where did you receive the information you needed to know for your tests?* Students nearly unanimously answer that their teachers were their primary information sources. Students' expectations that their teachers' inputs will also serve as the outcomes continues in college.

In my observations of college students doing various types of academic work, during individual and group study sessions, it's evident that they heavily rely on their class notes. Whether these artifacts consist of PowerPoint notes that have been distributed in class or online, or whether students have extracted the material from class, they depend on the content educators cover *during class*. Despite the amount of time they spend studying, their focus remains on memorizing, reformatting, or completing their notes. This reliance on surface-level learning and memorization can lead to the 80/20 trap, where students spend 80% of their time on low-value microlabor tasks and only 20% on high-value macrolabor tasks.

Many students enter college within an 80/20 perspective on academic work. They believe that 80% of learning occurs during class, and that they should have a clear understanding of the material presented before they leave. This perspective means that students view themselves as passive receivers of information, and that their primary goal is to memorize and reformat notes taken during class. They see their role in knowledge construction as only about 20%, consisting of various methods to inventory information presented during class. This dynamic is especially evident in group study sessions, where students spend most of their time ensuring that they have captured the material covered during class. However, this approach is not suitable for college-level work, where learning is deep, complex, and nuanced, and requires active knowledge construction.

Students are unaware of a significant shift in the learning dynamic that occurs when they transition from high school to college. In high school, students spent approximately seven to eight hours per day in class with their educators, whereas in college, this time is nearly cut in half to three to four hours per day. Consequently, college students are exposed to significantly less information in the classroom than they were in high school. However, students who fall into the 80/20 trap continue to try to extract 80% of the information from their college classrooms. As a result, they obtain a limited amount of information. When college students hear that a test is coming up, they are often bewildered because they feel they haven't learned enough to pass the test. This feeling of bewilderment is an early indicator of the 80/20 trap.

Mia, a sophomore student from the University of California at San Diego, described her 80/20 trap experience like this:

> Even though we had been in class for nearly a month, I was completely shocked when Dr. Kemp reminded us of our test that was coming up the next week. I remember looking through my notes, wondering if some pages were missing. After seeing all the class dates on my notes, I asked some of my classmates how they felt about the upcoming test. We all felt as if we did not have enough information to possibly be ready for the test.

A focus group I conducted in 2016, showed how the 80/20 trap can ensnare students without them realizing it. Here's an exchange from one of my focus group sessions.

Me: "You stated you were a successful high school student. When did you realize things were not working out in your college classes?"

Student 1: "I was surprised when I got my first round of test scores back. I thought I was prepared for the test, but I received the lowest grades I've ever received in my life. I've always been a straight-A student. But I had Ds and low Cs on all my exams."

Me: "What kinds of connections did you see between the tests and the material covered in class."

Student 1: "That's just it. I didn't see much connection. I saw words that my professors mentioned in class, but the tests were asking something different than what was presented in class."

Student 2: "I studied my class notes over and over again, but that didn't seem to help at all. I felt just as lost as if I had never studied."

Me: "Many of you have referenced studying material from your classes to prepare for your tests. What else did you do beyond that?"

At this point, many of the students looked bewildered and actively looked to each other to respond to the question. The students were unable to answer this question because, from their view, academic work consisted of paying attention in class and studying their notes. This is precisely the surface epistemic view of which researchers warned.

The 80/20 trap is rooted in a misconception about the nature of teaching and roles that the college teachers and students should play in the environment. Students' inflated view of the instruction that occurs inside the classroom causes them to abdicate their responsibility for working away from class. Indeed, when I ask students to list their sources in a hierarchy, they list their teachers first. This means that when these students hit the inevitable rough patches in learning, they go to their teachers first. On the surface, this may appear as good practice. However, I believe it indicates that students are not willing or able to try and figure things out independently. They pressure college professors to teach them the material a second and third time. Many college professors have been operating under these conditions for so long that they can't imagine things being another way.

When I began working with the natural sciences' division of a selective, liberal arts university in Ohio in 2018, the faculty reported that trying to live up to the university's focus on faculty accessibility was quite exhausting. Once I worked alongside them during the fall 2018 semester, I witnessed their plight firsthand. Watching them work exhausted me. With a student body focused on getting admitted to top graduate programs, the faculty darted back and forth from meetings with individual students, to supplemental instruction sessions, to student-professor research projects, not to mention their professional research and teaching loads.

When I informed the faculty that a decrease in their workloads would be a byproduct of the program I was installing, they looked at me in disbelief. Yet as we removed the functional traps from the environment, within a year the faculty were relishing their new, freer schedule. As one professor stated, "I've actually gotten my research work done ahead of schedule for the first time ever! I feel guilty, but my students have accepted their new roles and are thriving." Shifting students from an 80/20 view to a 20/80 view was the first and most fundamental shift. This paradigm shift helps focus students on doing academic work away from class.

The inflection point that triggered the changes was helping students shift from viewing themselves as information acquirers to knowledge producers. An information acquirer is a student who views the purpose of teaching as sharing information. No problem with this view. However, they also believe their sole purpose is to acquire information. Table 5.1 shows the condensed results of a survey we used to assess if students identified themselves as information acquirers or knowledge producers.

Clear fissures appeared after we asked students to identify the bullets that reflected their views and functions. The highest performing students had circled more responses in the knowledge producer column, while the middle performing students' responses skewed toward the information acquirer column, with a few responses lining up with one or two items in the knowledge producer column. However, all the responses of the lowest performing students aligned with the information acquirer column.

Making these differences in viewpoints and practices explicitly clear was more effective than other support efforts, such as reteaching, mentoring, tutoring, and so forth, that were common at the school. Furthermore, students were empowered because they saw that they did not lack the ability to do the work. Once they changed their views, classes became more engaging, learning was more rewarding, and overall performance improved. Here's a quote from Dr. Hefner, one of the professors at that institution:

> Students can now make connections between the individual details and the big picture of the course. Students see themselves as active partners in the educational process rather than passive recipients. I have noticed improved dynamics in the classroom, as well as more cohesive teamwork in the laboratory setting.

TABLE 5.1 Information Acquirer versus Knowledge Producer

Information Acquirer *80/20 View*	*Knowledge Producer* *20/80 View*
Sees the teacher as *the source* of information.	Seeks other sources to expand and further develop content *beyond the classroom.*
Believes gathering information is the only force that is needed.	Believes they are responsible for further developing information.
Considers studying their class notes as the bulk of studying activity.	Considers studying their class notes as the foundation of their studying activity.
Considers reading as studying.	Separates reading from studying.

Building Frameworks to Avoid Functional Traps

New college students may struggle to adapt to the new college environment and professors because they automatically assimilate their college instructors and professors into their existing framework for teachers. To help them reconceptualize their college educator, it's important to encourage students to expand their view of what constitutes a teacher. Changing students' epistemic views is deeper than getting them to adopt new practices. It involves changing their core conceptions about what learning and academic work entails. If these misconceptions are not properly addressed, they can prevent students from learning properly. Frameworks act as filters for the abstract information students encounter. They are processing shortcuts that help them quickly understand information. When change students' framework, we change how they process information. Fortunately, changing students' framework is a natural function of the mind. Building on Piaget's seminal work on assimilation and accommodation (Piaget, 1980), students can either assimilate, integrate, or expand their existing framework about how they and their teachers should function in college. Here's a description of how we can recognize how students are handling their encounters with you.

Assimilation

Students assimilate their experiences when they try to typecast you into their existing schema or mental models of what a teacher is like. The assume you will function like their previous teachers. This is the most common way students process encounters with college teachers. They expect the content and level of work to be harder in college, but they automatically expect you to function as their high school teacher did. This is precisely the way of thinking that led Bryce into the 80/20 Trap.

Integration

Students integrate their experiences when they create different categories for different types of teachers. To integrate properly, students should not categorize teachers by their discipline. Rather, they should categorize them by the roles they perform in academic work. For example, students should know whether the inputs of information you provide during instruction will match the outcomes that you are assessing. This foreknowledge will set clear expectations about your roles and inform them of the roles they must take on to properly learn the material. You know your students are integrating when they expand their understanding of what a teacher can be like and develop a more nuanced understanding of the teaching profession.

Accommodation

Finally, for many students, the college teachers they encounter will not fit neatly into their existing schema or mental models. In these cases, they will need to expand their existing understanding by creating new schema or modifying existing ones to fit the new way their teachers' function, and by establishing a new understanding of their teachers, students also establish new roles and responsibilities for themselves as learners. For example, if a student now understands their professor will expect them to learn material even if it was not explicitly addressed during class, then the students will have to use the course syllabus to ensure they are learning the required content. When I shared the 20/80 paradigm with Bryce, I was providing a new schema for him to process the academic environment. Once he began to view class from this perspective, he had a clearer division of labor. He understood where his teacher's labor stopped and his began.

Since I presented the 20/80 paradigm in 2012, hundreds of college and high school teachers have contacted me to express how useful the new understanding has been to them. Here are some quotes taken directly from the article posting.

I liked the explanation of 80/20 rule being reversed to the 20/80 rule by moving from high school to college. Understanding the way the professor is presenting the information and how to obtain information needed are very important variables in maximizing learning.

Calvin Matthews

Teaching at a community college I find most of the students are imbedded in the 80/20 rule. The second thing is they are very insecure about what they know and what they think they know! It is not lack of desire but lack of confidence. I plan on using this article for a workshop with other faculty in the near future. Thanks for the article!!

M. Newton

This article describes me to a "T." I was a "good" student in high school and I never really had to study too much. I'm having trouble trying to find a way of studying that fits me best and reflects good grades. I think that the 80/20; 20/80 idea is great. I know that a lot of what my teachers discuss is explained more in the book. Fifty minutes is just not enough time to elaborate on topics. Generally, the book is where all of the answers are and I struggle trying to figure out how to read textbooks and be well prepared for tests. I'm so excited for this study and cannot wait to become a GREAT student!

Alex Griffin

This article was incredible. It definitely gave me a different outlook on how to view a 'great learner' versus a 'good learner.' I wish I would have read this article before my semester started, but it is something I can always apply to my studies from here on out. The funny part is I have always put so much time and effort into my studies and received nothing higher than a 'B' but the person beside me barely studies and aces the test. Now I understand why based off the facts about 80/20 and 20/80 learning. Thank you for providing a solution and explanation to help improve our work/study habits!

Kandace

These students and educators are expressing how blissful teaching and learning can be when students switch from an outdated 80/20 paradigm to a 20/80 paradigm. The article helped them accommodate a better understanding of what college teachers are like, leading to a more nuanced and sophisticated understanding of the teaching profession.

Question and Exercise for Teachers

- Reflect on your days as a student and you perhaps encountered a teacher whose expectations did not fit your existing framework. How did you discover their expectations? How did you react to this new experience? Did you use assimilation, integration, or accommodation to make sense of it? Describe your experience with adapting to the new style? How can you use your experience to help your students understand your teaching framework?
- Imagine that you have a student who claims to be studying hard, but their grades are poor. How can you use the Information Acquirer vs. Knowledge Producer Table to shift the students view of academic work?
- Think about a time when you had to expand your existing framework to accommodate new information or experiences. How did this expansion help you better understand the world around you?
- Consider a student in your class who complains that you are trying to "trick" them by expecting students to know things on tests that were not covered during class. What strategies could you use to help them make connections between new and old information?

- Assume you have clearly explained the knowledge producer role to a student, but the student is resistant to changing how they function. How could you help them overcome their resistance and integrate the new information into their framework?

Exercise

Divide the class into small groups and ask each group to compare one of the Information Acquirer views with a Knowledge Producer view. Have each group discuss the steps they would take to adopt the Knowledge Producer view. Then, have each group present their steps to the class and lead a discussion about the different strategies that could be used to help them function as knowledge producers.

6

PEDAGOGICAL BELIEFS TRAP

Students' epistemological views serve as the foundation of their pedagogical beliefs, which shape their understanding of learning and influence their expectations of educators. While views and beliefs are often conflated, it is crucial to differentiate them because unraveling students' beliefs is the key to accessing their underlying views. By distinguishing epistemological views from pedagogical beliefs, we gain insight into how students perceive the process of learning.

Viewing, in its essence, is prethinking and prejudgment. Students assume their perspective on learning is the only valid one until confronted with contrasting views. However, these contrasting views are often initially perceived as differing beliefs rather than alternative perspectives. This brings us to the realm of pedagogical beliefs.

Students' pedagogical beliefs are derived from their observations and experiences, influencing what they see, hear, and ultimately believe about effective teaching practices. To illustrate this interconnectedness, let me share a personal example. My wife does not prefer driving. So, by the time my son reached the age of 11 years old, he had only witnessed me driving whenever our family traveled together. Unbeknownst to us, the repeated pattern of watching me drive had quietly instilled a belief in my son that the husband always drives the wife around. It was not until he encountered a situation where a woman was driving her husband that his belief, and viewpoint, came to light. As he witnessed the wife assuming the driver's seat while her husband sat beside her in the passenger's seat, my son blurted out, "Is Charles (the husband) sick? Why isn't he driving?"

DOI: 10.4324/9781003447252-8

Subsequently, he approached my wife and conveyed his belief that men should always be the ones driving women around. It was in this moment that my wife enlightened him, revealing her distaste for driving and clarifying that she only did so when necessary. This incident highlighted the fact that my son's specific belief had formed based on a broader view he had unconsciously absorbed regarding the dynamics of husband-wife driving roles. The consistent observations he made had cast me as "the driver" and my wife as "the passenger" within his mental framework. What's more, he generalized these roles to encompass all heterosexual couples, assuming that any deviation from these preconceived roles indicated something was amiss with the husband.

This embedded general view, which dictated that men should be the drivers when accompanied by women, and the corresponding specific belief that Charles should have been driving his wife, had firmly stereotyped men and women into predefined roles within my son's perception. Interestingly, neither my son nor we had realized that this mental structure had taken shape in his mind, silently influencing his outlook, until he was confronted with an alternative perspective. The introduction of this differing viewpoint compelled him to articulate his belief, thereby allowing all of us to peer through the lens of his belief and gain insight into his viewpoint.

Recognizing the interplay between views and beliefs is crucial because true liberation of students requires an epistemological shift. However, the most effective entry point to achieve this shift is through their beliefs. Therefore, in this chapter, we focus on the pedagogical beliefs that stem from students' epistemological views.

Students' academic pedagogy encompasses their beliefs regarding how educators should teach and how students should learn. Like my son, students unconsciously internalize a viewpoint on learning that becomes their default understanding of academic environments. This viewpoint shapes their current beliefs about effective teaching methods and student learning approaches. These views and beliefs are deeply intertwined and are either continuously reinforced or challenged.

To summarize, students' epistemic views refer to their perspective on what learning entails, while their pedagogical beliefs encompass their beliefs and practices regarding how educators should teach and facilitate learning. Both factors significantly impact students' experiences with educators, academic material, and learning environments, influencing their interactions with teachers, engagement levels, and motivation both inside and outside the classroom. For instance, a student with an 80/20 epistemic view of learning will likely believe that knowledge is transmitted directly from the teacher to the student, without much knowledge construction work away from class. Consequently, they may rely on rote memorization as a study strategy, feeling disengaged during class and assuming they can memorize the material later. If assessment material deviates from the daily class content, they may perceive the teaching as unsatisfactory. Conversely, a student with a 20/80 lens will recognize the teacher's role in providing foundational information in class and expect to actively construct their knowledge outside of class. This student is more likely to actively participate in class, seeking the right inputs to enhance their learning. As a result, they will be better prepared for assessments that measure deeper understanding.

As demonstrated, students' views and beliefs directly influence their engagement, motivation, and willingness to participate in classroom activities and discussions. Understanding the relationship between students' views and beliefs sets the stage for exploring how these pedagogical beliefs translate into roles in the next section.

The Sequence to Changing Students' Behavior

Let's analyze Bryce's statements in light of our newfound understanding of epistemic views and beliefs.

> My professor is terrible! I feel like I'm wasting my money here [at the college]. She goes over all this material in class and none of it is ever on her tests. I'll do the work. She just needs to tell me what I need to know.

Bryce's declaration that his professor is "terrible" is not a personal attack but rather a judgment of her job performance, stemming from his pedagogical beliefs about how teachers should function.

The subsequent statement, "I feel like I'm wasting my money here," reveals Bryce's overarching epistemic views. He perceives his professor's shortcomings as devaluing his educational experience. However, the real essence of the functional trap becomes evident in the following three sentences.

Bryce's complaint that the material covered in class does not align with the content of the tests exposes the core expectation that lies at the heart of all functional traps: a misaligned expectation. Bryce expects his professor's class presentations to directly prepare him for the tests in the course. He seeks a direct correlation between the content presented in class and the content on which he will be assessed. When his professor fails to meet this expectation, he deems her incapable and regards the time spent in class as a waste of money. At this point, Bryce's outdated epistemic view of his professor only vaguely surfaces. However, it becomes more evident in his final sentence when he articulates his belief about what his professor should do.

Bryce's concluding statement explicitly unveils his pedagogical belief regarding his professor's role: "She just needs to tell me what I need to know." He firmly believes that educators should provide students with precise information that will be mirrored on assessments. In fact, he considers it their primary responsibility. Although college professors may find Bryce's expectation absurd, it aligns with the role that his pre-college educators consistently played. Bryce is experiencing what cognitive scientists refer to as functional fixedness, a cognitive condition in which previous knowledge of how something worked in the past can hinder the recognition of its potential in new contexts (American Psychological Association, 2021). From this perspective, Bryce's expectation is entirely logical, as it is derived from the data accumulated through his educational experiences up to this point in his life.

However, the most significant line in Bryce's statement is his declaration, "I'll do the work." He expressed this with conviction, assuring me of his willingness to do his part while presuming that the professor will fulfill her part. He signifies his commitment to putting in the effort required, whatever it may entail.

But how can Bryce claim he will do the work while also desiring his professor to provide him with all the necessary information for the tests? This apparent conflict is the essence of a functional trap. Bryce has typecast both his professor and himself into roles depicted in Table 6.1.

Observe the relationships between each of the professor's roles and each of Bryce's roles. The role Bryce assigns to himself complements his perception of how his professor should function. If the professor were to fulfill Bryce's expectations, he would likely excel in the course. However, when the professor fails to meet these expectations, Bryce persists in trying to

TABLE 6.1 Bryce's Typecast Roles

Professor's Roles	Bryce's Roles
Presenter: educators are supposed to present the important information.	Observer: students are supposed be attentive in class and capture all the information that is covered.
Reinforcer: educators are supposed to use activities, assignments, and so forth to reinforce the material covered during class.	Recorder: students are supposed to apply themselves to learn as much of the information covered during class as possible.
Assessor: educators use tests to assess how much and how well students grasp the content that was covered during class.	Reproducer: students should be able to fully and fluidly recall the information that was covered during class.

adhere to his assumed roles. They both become trapped. Bryce will only break free from this trap when he recognizes that he has typecasted both himself and his professor.

Recognizing that students are ensnared in functional traps requires educators to listen deeply to students' words rather than reacting solely to their emotions. I could have taken offense at Bryce's concise description of my colleague. However, by suppressing my emotions, I was able to listen beyond the surface and discern the underlying issue he was communicating. This insight enabled me to identify the functional trap that was impeding his academic performance. Detecting functional traps is challenging because we must work backward from students' behaviors, navigate their emotionally charged beliefs, and delve into their underlying views. Then, we must comprehend how these beliefs and views manifest as roles.

Let's explore how views, beliefs, and roles interact. Students' epistemological views are deeply ingrained in their minds and shape how they perceive events within the learning environment. Their pedagogical beliefs are expressed through their words, and attentive listening allows us to detect these beliefs as they discuss how they and others function within the learning environment. Students' views and beliefs manifest in the roles they assign to themselves and others throughout the learning process. These roles are worth examining because students often typecast themselves into roles that are incompatible with the roles they need to fulfill in college. This misperception of how teachers should teach them hampers their own ability to learn effectively.

Typecasting Educators

Combining students' epistemological views and pedagogical beliefs results in a typecast of educators and students. This concept of typecasting originates from creating impressions for replication (Merriam-Webster, 2019). Students rely on the typecast of their high school educators to understand expectations and their relationship with them. These mental models persist into college. When educators deviate from the typecasted role, students feel something is amiss. Typecasts are reciprocal, shaping how students perceive their own roles based on their beliefs about educators' roles. Bryce's experience exemplifies this. He expected his professor to provide the necessary information, defining his role as studying what the teacher instructed. However, when the professor didn't meet this expectation, Bryce felt lost and trapped. Table 6.1 illustrates the typecast roles for Bryce and his professor.

Typecasting traps individuals into prescribed roles, whether at work or within families, often unconsciously accepting and assigning unsolicited roles. We realize we've typecasted someone when they deviate from

TABLE 6.2 Professor's Typecast Roles

Professor's Role	Student's Role
Presenter: educators are supposed to present salient course content.	Observer: students are supposed be attentive in class and capture all the information that is covered.
Reinforcer: educators are not responsible for reinforcing class content.	Constructer: Students are supposed to develop the information presented during class when they are away from class.
Assessor: educators use tests to assess what students can do with the information required for the course, regardless of whether it was explicitly covered.	Thinker: Students should be able to provide responses to questions and problems that are based upon—but not necessarily the same as—information that was covered during class.

their expected role, resulting in frustration and unexplained anger rooted in implicit expectations. Although the functional roles Bryce assigned to his college educators and himself were formalized during high school, they became apparent during the "Discover Your Roles" exercise reflected in Table 6.1. It revealed that Bryce's harsh judgment of his professor was based on three specific roles he expected her to fulfill. Bryce calibrated his roles to complement hers, believing he fulfilled all his responsibilities, placing the problem on his professor. When I informed the professor that one of her hardworking students believed she was terrible at her job, she initially felt sad, then angry. She vented her frustration against students she believed shouldn't be in college. Without knowing the student's identity, she constructed a complete profile, assuming poor behavior. This imaginary typecasting led her to believe that if a student deemed her terrible, they must be incompetent. She had typecasted Bryce, overlooking his exemplary performance. Functional traps affect not only students but also faculty. Bryce's professor operated within her own functional roles depicted in Table 6.2.

The professor's assumption that Bryce would accurately recall the information presented in class was not remarkable; it was the expected norm. It's akin to receiving a new car with tires already installed—nothing impressive, just a standard feature. College educators typically evaluate students based on the knowledge they have constructed from the provided class information. (Methods for assisting students in constructing knowledge will be explored in the Cognitive Traps section.) Similarly, the professor established her functional roles to align with the unspoken roles she anticipated students to fulfill. Table 6.3 illustrates the implicit understanding of roles held by both Bryce and the professor.

It's clear upon examining these roles that Bryce and his professor held contrasting epistemological and pedagogical perspectives. The professor's

TABLE 6.3

Bryce's Typecast Roles		Professor's Typecast Roles	
Professor's Roles	*Bryce's Roles*	*Professor's Role*	*Student's Role*
Presenter: educators are supposed to present the important information.	Observer: students are supposed to be attentive in class and capture all the information that is covered.	Presenter: educators are supposed to present salient course content.	Observer: students are supposed be attentive in class and capture all the information that is covered.
Reinforcer: educators are supposed to use activities, assignments, and so forth to reinforce the material covered during class.	Recorder: students are supposed to apply themselves to learn as much of the information covered during class as possible.	Reinforcer: educators are not responsible for reinforcing class content.	Constructer: Students are supposed to develop the information presented during class when they are away from class.
Assessor: educators use tests to assess how much and how well students grasp the content that was covered during class.	Reproducer: students should be able to fully and fluidly recall the information that was covered during class.	Assessor: educators use tests to assess what students can do with the information required for the course, regardless of whether it was explicitly covered.	Thinker: Students should be able to provide responses to questions and problems that are based upon—but not necessarily the same as—information that was covered during class.

deep understanding of learning, instructional beliefs, and predefined expectations of college educators and students collided with Bryce's superficial perception of learning, studying approach, and preconceived notions of college dynamics. Put simply, both of them found themselves entangled in functional traps!

With this understanding of their predicament, we now transition to the best method for aligning students epistemic views and pedagogical beliefs with their teachers: helping them develop a new academic vision.

7
THE POWER OF ACADEMIC VISION

The eye is like a lamp that provides light for your body. When your eye is healthy, your whole body is filled with light. But when your eye is unhealthy, your whole body is filled with darkness. And if the light you think you have is actually darkness, how deep is that darkness?

– Matthew 6:22–23

This profound passage vividly demonstrates the power of vision and its influence on our perception of the world. Just as navigating without sight is challenging, believing we have sight when we don't is deceitful and perilous. In the realm of education, students are guided by their academic vision. However, if their vision remains superficial while their teachers possess a deeper understanding, reconciling their differences becomes an insurmountable task. This manner of misaligned vision creates functional traps. Breaking free from these traps demands that students develop a fresh, new vision for their academic environment, their teachers and academic work.

When we transform students' academic vision, we fundamentally alter their perception of the countless elements, interactions, and experiences that encompass their academic journey. Although this transformation may pose challenges, it is an essential step towards achieving alignment and liberating us and our students from functional traps. If students persist in viewing their college environment through the lens of their past, they risk misinterpreting crucial elements and situations, resulting in restricted learning and hindered

DOI: 10.4324/9781003447252-9

performance. To illustrate how an outdated vision can cause us to misread present interactions, consider the following passage:

> Time flies like an arrow.
> Fruit flies like a banana.

The word "like" is used in two distinct contexts, yet our brains automatically apply the first context to the second sentence, leading to a misinterpretation. So instead of reading the second sentence as "fruit flies like eating a banana," we read it as "fruit flies through the air like a banana." And we read it this way, even though it doesn't make sense (Wikipedia, 2022). Upon closer analysis of how our brains were deceived, we can observe that the first sentence employs the word "like" as a simile, drawing a comparison between the swift passage of time and an arrow swiftly traversing through the air. This establishes a mental framework for how our brain processes the same word in the subsequent sentence. However, the context shifts in this sentence, leading our brain to mistakenly interpret the second sentence based on an outdated understanding of the word. Consequently, our brain becomes ensnared in this outdated usage, resulting in an erroneous interpretation of the second sentence. This serves as a reminder that our academic vision operates similarly. As students embark on their college journey, they often possess a superficial academic vision, causing them to approach academic work with limited depth. While shallow vision may suffice in certain contexts, it becomes problematic when most college teachers possess a deeper vision of academic rigor and inquiry.

Exploring Conflicting Academic Visions

Now, let us delve into the impact of conflicting academic visions on students' learning. To illustrate this, consider two students, Shemeka and Dwayne, faced with the same test question and subsequent follow-up questions. Table 7.1 demonstrates how students' academic visions can initially support them in high school but ultimately ensnare them in college, hindering their academic progress and success.

Suppose Shemeka finds herself in a class where the teacher prioritizes shallow responses, such as recalling dates and names of key figures in historical events. Being a diligent student, she has excelled in this approach and developed a surface-level academic vision. However, when she enters college, her history professor poses a question about a different war, expecting a deeper understanding. Shemeka applies her usual process and provides shallow information, unaware that her professor operates from a deep

TABLE 7.1 Surface Vision versus Deep Vision

Surface Shemeka	Deep Dwayne
Q1: What was the date of the battle of the Spanish Armada? *A: 1588* Q2: How do you know this? *A: It was one of the dates I memorized for the exam.*	Q1: What was the date of the battle of the Spanish Armada? *A: It must have been around 1590.* Q2: How do you know this? *A: I know the English began to settle in Virginia just after 1600, although I'm not sure of the exact date. They wouldn't have dared start overseas explorations if Spain still had control of the seas. It would have taken a little while to get expeditions organized, so England must have gained naval supremacy somewhere in the late 1500s.*
Q3: Why is the event important? *A: I don't know.*	Q3: Why is the event important? *A: It marks a turning point in the relative importance of England and Spain as European powers and colonizers of the New World.*

Source: National Research Council, 2000.

academic vision. As a result, her responses fall short, leading to lower scores than she anticipated.

In contrast, Dwayne adopts a comprehensive approach to the subject. Although he may not recall the exact date of the conflict, he demonstrates a broader understanding of the topic compared to Shemeka. However, let's imagine that Dwayne's professor specifically emphasizes precise dates. Since he cannot provide the exact date, the assessment may incorrectly suggest that Dwayne lacks knowledge of the content, despite grasping its essence.

This is where educators play a crucial role. Research indicates that it is educators, rather than the discipline or the course itself, who determine the appropriate approach warranted (Eklund-Myrkog, 1997, Nelson, 2008). It is essential to emphasize this point because a widespread misconception exists in higher education. Educators and students often wrongly attribute the difficulty of a course to the discipline itself. For instance, STEM courses are considered more challenging than humanities courses, or higher-level courses are presumed to be more difficult than lower-level ones. This misconception reflects a lack of understanding regarding the factors that dictate the level of challenge in a course. In reality, it is the educator who determines the level of challenge. As I often demonstrate in workshops, a cake-baking course can present greater cognitive complexity than a quantum physics course. The academic field, course title, or content do not inherently determine a course's difficulty. In the upcoming Cognitive Traps unit, we will explore how difficulty is influenced by the level of cognitive complexity set by the educator.

Returning to our example with Shemeka and Dwayne, if Shemeka's instructor assessed for exactness (e.g., precise dates), she would likely perform well, but the academic challenge would be low. (It is important to note that exactness is not unimportant, but it can be achieved through diligent rote memorization skills, which align with a surface vision of academic work.) On the other hand, if Dwayne were in the same class, he might receive a lower grade than Shemeka, despite having a deeper understanding of the material.

Conversely, if the same material were presented in a class where the educator valued thoroughness and depth of knowledge, the outcomes would be reversed. Dwayne would excel, while Shemeka would face difficulties. The key point to remember is that educators' vision, whether deep or surface, significantly influences what students learn, how they learn it, and their overall performance.

By examining the influence of academic vision on students' learning journeys, we gain valuable insights into the importance of cultivating a deep, compatible vision between teachers and students. Now that we have a greater appreciation for the profound role that vision plays in academic settings, we now can explore strategies to bridge the gap between differing visions and foster an environment that is free from functional traps.

Changing Students' Academic Vision

Academic vision refers to the lens through which students perceive and interpret academic experiences. It encompasses their beliefs about learning and their role as learners. Research indicates three types of academic visions commonly found among students: surface, deep, and strategic (Nelson, 2008).

Surface Vision

A surface vision is rooted in a passive approach to learning. Students operating from this perspective rely heavily on memorization techniques without establishing meaningful connections between the material and achieving academic success. They often harbor fears of failure and lack the drive for innovative and creative thinking. Consequently, their work tends to be average, and they struggle to attain grades higher than Cs in courses that demand critical thinking and deep understanding (Flippo & Caverly, 2009). For example, a nursing student with a surface vision may focus primarily on memorizing historical facts, names, and dates in a history course. Similarly, in their nursing classes, they would meticulously record every issue and trend covered in lectures and textbooks. Their study efforts would revolve around storing, organizing, and recalling information. While these skills may prove useful in less cognitively challenging tasks, they fall short when faced with demanding academic assignments. To determine whether students have a surface vision, consider the following checklist:

- Do students focus solely on memorizing information instead of understanding it?
- Do they engage in learning solely to pass exams or meet deadlines?
- Do they rely solely on the teacher for answers without exploring the material independently?
- Do they ask only test-related questions?
- Do they shy away from exploring new or unfamiliar topics that challenge them?

Deep Vision

A deep vision aligns with rigorous learning environments. Students with a deep vision strive to derive meaning from the information they encounter. They seek to establish connections between ideas and concepts, fostering holistic understanding. Deep learners often recognize interconnections across different academic disciplines. For instance, a nursing student concurrently taking an American history course might enhance their learning by applying the historians' approach to determining salient information in their field to identify the most relevant contemporary issues and trends in nursing. The ability to extract salience lessons from the history domain and connect them to nursing demonstrates the presence of a deep vision. Students with a deep vision not only perform well academically but also develop as sophisticated learners.

To determine whether students have a deep vision, consider the following checklist:

- Do students display genuine interest in the subject matter and actively seek additional information?
- Do they connect new information with their existing knowledge to develop a deeper understanding?
- Do they question the material and explore alternative explanations?
- Do they attempt to apply what they have learned to real-life situations?
- Do they demonstrate comprehension by explaining the material to others?

Strategic Vision

Students with a strategic vision exhibit a flexible approach, shifting between deep and surface visions depending on the perceived demands of each course. These ambidextrous learners may engage passively in non-major courses to merely "get through" them, while investing more effort in their major-related courses. For instance, a nursing student may employ deep learning strategies in nursing courses but resort to surface-level tactics in a history course.

However, students with a strategic vision may unintentionally hinder their own progress. Their choice of adopting a deep or surface vision is often based on whether the course falls within their major, which is an inadequate metric for determining the appropriate vision. It is essential to emphasize that the educator, rather than the course or discipline, determines the suitable vision for each course. For example, I once collaborated with a school to enhance their first-year seminar course. The course transitioned from a one-credit "college knowledge" class to a six-credit reading and writing-intensive course. Since it was a first-year course outside students' majors, many assumed they could rely solely on memorization. Unfortunately, these students were mistaken, resulting in exceedingly low midterm grades. Surprisingly, many students who struggled in the first-year course excelled in historically challenging courses like chemistry, math, and physics. Focus group data revealed that they unknowingly employed a deep vision in the courses they deemed "difficult." However, their misconceptions about the first-year course automatically triggered a surface vision. But once we help students understand the nature of the course and differentiate between surface and deep visions, they shifted their approach, and the mean score in this first-year seminar course improved.

To assess whether students are adopting a strategic approach, you can utilize the checklist questions for both surface and deep visions on a class-specific basis. However, it's important to recognize that students are prone to misjudging when they should employ surface or deep learning methods.

When considering students' academic vision, two crucial points should be understood by both students and educators:

1 The educator determines the approach: Both parties must refrain from assuming which approach is required based solely on the academic discipline, course level, or amount of course material. While these factors can influence the approach, they do not dictate it.

2 The interaction between educators' and students' approaches: Educators who can identify whether students' academic work stems from a surface, deep, or strategic vision have a significant advantage over their peers who

lack this understanding. They can assist students in transitioning to a vision that aligns better with the course requirements.

Ultimately, students are influenced by what they perceive. Their vision, whether it is surface, deep, or strategic, plays a critical role in shaping how they learn and what they learn.

Educators play a vital role in molding students' vision. By assessing their vision and clearly communicating how they themselves function and what they expect from students, educators can prevent the inadvertent establishment of functional traps and help students break free from them. Dr. Kaiser provides an exemplary model in this regard.

Escaping Functional Traps

In 2014, I had the opportunity to meet Dr. Kaiser, a psychology professor at a liberal arts university in rural Kentucky, who humorously referred to himself as "the parrot keeper." When I asked him why he referred to himself in this manner, he said, "Because that's what I do. I teach students who simply echo my words, and I'm constantly having to clean up their crap." Clearly, this nickname stemmed from his frustration with students who merely regurgitated information without critical thinking. Dr. Kaiser's struggle became evident during my investigation of his online integrated studies course, which combined psychology and religion.

Despite Dr. Kaiser's intention of fostering deep conversations and exploration of psychology and religion, the students' journal entries, which made up the bulk of the course's submitted work, consisted of distorted paraphrases rather than meaningful engagement. Disappointed with their lack of critical thinking, Dr. Kaiser contemplated discontinuing the course. However, after discovering this functional trap, I proposed a solution: interviewing his students and providing feedback.

During my interviews with the students, I uncovered differing perspectives regarding their lower-than-expected journal submission scores. Some believed Dr. Kaiser's expectations were unclear, while others thought they should have cited him or other sources more extensively. Surprisingly, the students were focused on providing "the right answers" rather than delving into in-depth discussions.

Dr. Kaiser and his students found themselves entangled in two functional traps. First, they mistakenly approached the course with the 80/20 paradigm and second, they unwittingly confined Dr. Kaiser and themselves within the confines of outdated high school teacher-student dynamics. This ultimately resulted in a dysfunctional relationship. The students had embraced a surface vision, influenced by their prior experiences in high school where regurgitating information word-for-word held significant value. On the other hand, Dr. Kaiser envisioned a classroom environment characterized by profound interactions and critical thinking. Unfortunately, neither side was aware of the underlying issue, leading to confusion and questioning of each other's abilities and intentions.

To address this, we devised a plan. First, Dr. Kaiser asked the students to reflect on their academic vision while writing their previous journals, identifying areas where they could have approached the work from a deep vision. Then, he requested that they rewrite and resubmit new journal entries based on this deep vision. The results were remarkable—students not only demonstrated deeper expressions of thought but also engaged in thoughtful discussions with one another.

This process liberated the students from their functional traps, proving that they were not incapable of quality work but rather trapped in ineffective approaches. Dr. Kaiser's enjoyment of the class was rekindled, and he realized the immense potential in his students.

To replicate these outcomes, I propose the following instructional steps:

- Step 1: Cast a new vision. Clearly communicate to students that an alternative academic vision exists—one that encourages deep thinking and engagement.
- Step 2: Help students make the right choice. Present the deep academic work vision as the most effective option, emphasizing the benefits of improved studying, time management, and increased engagement.
- Step 3: Reinforce the new vision. Seize opportunities to reinforce the deep vision through positive feedback and acknowledgment of students' deep thinking efforts.
- Step 4: Expect regression, but don't settle for it. Anticipate occasional setbacks as students may revert to their surface vision habits. Instead of viewing this as a limitation, reorient them to the deep vision and remind them of the class's foundations.
- Step 5: Repeat. Implement this process at the beginning of each course to prevent functional traps and enable students to experience the rewards of academic work.

As I concluded my work with Dr. Kaiser, he eagerly looked forward to continuing his teaching career, using this tactic in all his courses until his retirement three years later. It brings me satisfaction to know that I played a part in helping Dr. Kaiser end his 30-year professorship with some of his most rewarding work.

Assessment Questions to Assess Students' Academic Vision

1 Do you primarily focus on memorizing information or seek to understand it deeply?
2 How do you approach learning: as a means to pass exams or as an opportunity to gain comprehensive knowledge?
3 Do you actively seek out additional information and resources related to the subject matter?
4 Are you able to make connections between different concepts and ideas across disciplines?
5 Do you question and critically analyze the material, seeking alternative explanations or perspectives?
6 Can you apply what you have learned to real-life situations and make practical connections?
7 Do you engage in discussions and debates with classmates to enhance your understanding?
8 Are you able to explain complex concepts in your own words and teach them to others?
9 How do you respond to challenging or unfamiliar topics? Do you embrace them as opportunities for growth or avoid them?
10 Are you willing to go beyond the requirements of the course and explore additional resources independently?

Exercises to Help Students Develop a Deep Academic Vision

1 Reflective Journaling: Encourage students to regularly reflect on their learning experiences, highlighting connections they've made, questions that arise, and areas where they can deepen their understanding.
2 Socratic Discussions: Conduct class discussions using the Socratic method, where students are encouraged to ask thought-provoking questions, challenge assumptions, and engage in critical analysis of the material.
3 Research Projects: Assign research projects that require students to delve deeper into a specific topic, analyze various sources, and synthesize information to develop a comprehensive understanding.
4 Collaborative Learning: Foster collaborative learning environments where students work together in groups to explore complex problems or case studies, encouraging them to think critically and share their perspectives.
5 Real-World Applications: Incorporate real-world applications of the subject matter into the curriculum, providing opportunities for students to apply their knowledge and see the relevance of what they are learning.

6 Problem-Based Learning: Present students with authentic, real-life problems or scenarios that require them to think critically, analyze information, and propose innovative solutions.

7 Debate and Argumentation: Organize debates or argumentation exercises where students can engage in structured discussions, presenting arguments, countering viewpoints, and developing a deeper understanding of complex issues.

8 Reflection and Peer Feedback: Integrate reflection exercises and peer feedback sessions into the learning process, encouraging students to assess their own work, provide constructive feedback to their peers, and identify areas for improvement.

9 Independent Research and Reading: Encourage students to pursue independent research and reading beyond the assigned course materials, fostering a habit of seeking out additional resources and expanding their knowledge.

10 Faculty Mentorship: Establish opportunities for students to engage in one-on-one mentorship or consultation sessions with faculty members, where they can discuss their academic goals, seek guidance, and receive feedback on their progress towards developing a deep academic vision.

SECTION III

Cognitive Traps

If you or your kids have played sports, then you likely are familiar with the phrase "the game within the game." This expression captures the idea that within the broader game being played, there exists a smaller, more focused game. Coaches employ this notion to empower their players by directing their attention towards aspects of the game they can control. For instance, a basketball coach might urge their team to hustle back on defense, aiming to limit the opponent's fast breaks. The underlying belief is that by restricting the opponent's easy points, victory in the game becomes more likely. Similarly, a soccer coach may stress the importance of maintaining team spacing as the crucial game to secure overall triumph. Meanwhile, a football coach might emphasize winning the turnover battle as the key to winning the entire contest. Essentially, the expression suggests that conquering the immediate battles will lead to victory in the ultimate war.

Did you know that students have learned to play a game within a game when it comes to academics? Throughout their pre-college education, students become skilled at playing the mental-matching game. They invest their time in amassing a wealth of information in their mental storehouses and employ various tactics to enhance the retrievability of these items. The premise of the game is that if they can effectively store and retrieve this information, they will perform well on assessments covering that material. It's the game within the game.

High school teachers inadvertently act as coaches in the mental-matching game. Their expertise in distilling information and making content more manageable, as exemplified in the Structural Traps and Functional Traps sections of this book, enables students to participate in this game. However,

DOI: 10.4324/9781003447252-10

the very strategies that lead students to success in the pre-college academic game set them up for failure in college. They enter college with firmly ingrained game rules in their minds, only to encounter a sudden shift in the rules of engagement. Unexpectedly, the skills they have mastered and the expertise they have acquired are rendered obsolete. Their perspective on academic work, which no longer aligns with the new challenges they face, and their practices that fall short of the new expectations, leave them ensnared in cognitive traps.

Cognitive Traps Introduction

Cognitive traps encompass the unforeseen disparities between the ways students used their minds to do academic work before college and how they must use their minds to do academic work during college. This uncharted gap between their previous modes of thinking and learning and the ones required in the present inhibits students from fully utilizing their academic potential in college. Even if students exert greater effort in college than ever before, cognitive traps will curtail their performance and undermine their potential.

When I contemplate cognitive traps, the story of Cole, a former student-worker in the convocation program at Lenoir-Rhyne University, comes to mind. As a student-employee, Cole exhibited an impressive work ethic. He was reliable, organized, consistently punctual, and took the initiative on work projects. I was particularly struck by how he utilized his downtime at work to study rather than wasting it on video games, social media, or streaming services.

I discovered that Cole began his college journey on a full academic scholarship after graduating with distinction from a prestigious private school. However, during his first year of college, Cole encountered an academic obstacle. Regardless of how much he studied, he could not achieve grades higher than Ds in his more challenging courses. These grades were utterly unacceptable to him, akin to receiving zeroes.

Embarrassed by his underperformance, Cole initially refrained from seeking help. Instead, he delved even deeper into studying. The most perplexing aspect of his experience was that he felt confident at the beginning of his exams. However, his confidence fluctuated throughout the test. Yet, when his professors reviewed the correct answers afterward, they resonated with him. Cole had numerous profound questions regarding his experience:

- Why did I feel so self-assured before the test? What formed the basis of my confidence?
- Why did I make so many seemingly straightforward mistakes while taking the test?

- Could I have developed test anxiety, as the school counselor suggested? This had never been an issue before.
- Most importantly, why did it seem like I knew the correct answers when my professor went over the test later on?

When I inquired about how Cole felt his prestigious private school had prepared him for college, he replied, "My school didn't teach us how to think. They only taught us how to outwork everyone else." This response offered profound insight. Cole's primary strategy for overcoming academic challenges had been sheer diligence. However, cognitive traps cannot be overcome through effort alone. Hard work becomes like quicksand when ensnared in a cognitive trap—the more one struggles, the deeper they sink.

Conditioned to Fail

Cognitive traps arise from the familiar mental-matching game that is prevalent among high school students. This game unfolds as follows: students cram their minds with as much information as possible, engage in what they perceive as studying, which primarily involves embedding mental cues for later recall of discrete facts. They then rely on the wording of test questions to trigger the desired information from their mental store. Once the test is completed, the information is promptly erased and rendered inaccessible. Such is the nature of the mental-matching game.

Jal Mehta and Sarah Fine, in their book, *In Search for Deeper Learning*, embarked on a research journey to thirty innovative public high schools and school districts celebrated for their exemplary practices in educating students from diverse socioeconomic backgrounds. They set out to explore how students in these institutions were engaging in profound thinking and learning. To their surprise, they found scant evidence of such cognitive work. Instead, they discovered that the level of cognition celebrated by evaluators at these schools lacked the depth that would typically be expected in college.

Using Bloom's Higher Order Thinking Skills as a framework for cognitive performance, Mehta and Fine established a continuum that placed tasks involving memorization and retrieval of information at the low-performance end, while tasks involving analysis, synthesis, and creativity were placed at the other end. The instructional environment and focus on low-level thinking fostered the mental-matching game that students learned to master. However, the memorization skills honed in these schools hindered the development of the deeper thinking modes required in college. Students eventually realize that the cognitive skills that helped them excel in high school are insufficient to thrive in college.

During their pre-college years, students not only acquire knowledge but also encode cognitive habits stored for future use. Researchers at The Graybiel Laboratory at Massachusetts Institute of Technology (MIT) have discovered that the human brain is inherently efficient (Graybiel, 1998, 2008). Whenever a cognitive skill is successfully employed, the brain stores it for future exploitation. When faced with similar conditions, the brain automatically activates the stored skill without conscious awareness. This process forms a "fixed-action unit," ultimately becoming a cognitive habit (Barnes, Kubota, Hu, & Dezne, 2005; Chersi, Mirolli, Pezzulo, & Baldassarre, 2013). While this habit formation typically aids us by freeing up mental capacity, it can work against us when the encoded skills differ from those required for current tasks—precisely the situation students find themselves in during college.

The predicament for students is that the ingrained learning habits they develop before college are incompatible with the thinking modes demanded in college. Thus, their previous strengths become weaknesses, resulting in cognitive traps.

How Cognitive Traps Affect Students

Cognitive traps are insidious obstacles that cause students to exert tremendous effort but yield unsatisfactory results. Throughout this section, you will encounter stories of diligent students who checked all the boxes of a good student but struggled due to their inability to recognize the required thinking processes and engage in the appropriate cognitive behaviors. Some students caught in these traps manage to navigate their way through college, but their performance remains mediocre. A metacognitive analysis reveals that many of these students lack clear learning goals, as discussed in the Structural Traps section. However, even if their teachers had provided explicit destinations for their work, these students would have been unable to reach them due to undifferentiated thinking skills. Consequently, they find themselves in a state of uncertainty, where they can only hope to have adequately prepared for exams. However, you will also encounter stories of students who break free from these cognitive traps and experience remarkable mental leaps, unlocking their true potential.

How Cognitive Traps Affect Educators

When students are trapped in cognitive traps, educators also become entangled. One of the primary indicators of cognitive traps is the proliferation of pseudowork. As you will discover in this section, pseudowork consumes our time with well-intentioned activities like reteaching and excessive office hours, but fails to produce desirable outcomes. These efforts steal valuable time and contribute to our sense of being overwhelmed.

I recall my collaboration with the natural science division of a prominent small college in Ohio from 2018 to 2020. The division aimed to address performance disparities among first-generation students and students of color, particularly in challenging first-year courses. Faculty members recognized the potential in these students, as many had excelled in high school. However, the performance gap between these students and their peers was undeniable. Initially, the faculty believed that a mentoring program pairing these students with successful peers would solve the problem. However, I persuaded them to establish a metacognitive-based Peer Learning Strategist program, which effectively eliminated cognitive traps. The program swiftly improved the performance of the targeted populations. Surprisingly, the strategies employed for these students proved beneficial for all students. One professor described the transformation, saying,

> There is now a more profound classroom experience for both students and myself ... students can connect individual details to the larger picture of the course. They view themselves as active partners in the learning process, not passive recipients. I have observed improved dynamics and cohesive teamwork in both introductory and advanced courses.

As an external observer, I noticed that by the end of my consultancy, the faculty perceived themselves as influential agents in enhancing student performance. The sense of empowerment and positivity was palpable. The faculty's instincts were accurate—their students were capable of far greater success than they had previously demonstrated. However, they needed to acquire a more sophisticated repertoire of cognitive skills to meet the demands of college work.

As Fitzgerald describes, many high school graduates accustomed to easy success face challenges in college. They encounter voluminous readings, comprehensive exams demanding untaught analysis, and papers requiring synthesis of ideas from multiple sources. Ill-equipped to handle the workload and the elevated cognitive demands, they fail (Fitzgerald, 2004).

The reality is that many students enter college with limited practice in utilizing sophisticated thinking skills or complex mental processes. They have relied on solid memorization, content organization techniques, and strong work ethic to navigate pre-college curricula. However, upon reaching college, they, like Cole, suddenly realize that something is different about the work they are expected to produce. A gap emerges between class content and the knowledge required for assessments, trapping students in cognitive dissonance. They discover that their problem-solving methods from the past, such as hard work and increased focus, no longer yield the desired results.

Fitzgerald's account highlights three common ways cognitive traps impact college students: *academic myopia*, *far transfer*, and *pseudowork*. These concepts are intricately connected. *Academic myopia* arises when students overly focus on the sheer amount of content, neglecting the broader concepts—a case of "seeing the trees, but not the forest." Their narrowed focus triggers shallow thinking, resulting in a mismatch between their thinking skills and the required ones, known as *far transfer*. Students trapped in far transfer struggle to meet performance standards set by educators. Consequently, they engage in *pseudowork*, a deceptive and futile type of academic effort that feels productive but hampers true learning. Students may spend significant time studying, note-taking, and reading, yet without the necessary metacognitive understanding, they substitute pseudowork for meaningful learning.

While cognitive traps remain invisible to students and educators, their presence can be detected through common frustrations expressed by stakeholders. For example, if you have encountered stakeholders expressing the following statements, then they are likely in the grip of cognitive traps.

- "My grades are not improving regardless of how much I study." (student)
- "I believe your tests are designed to trick me." (student)
- "Our students are not equipped to do the work we require of them." (faculty)
- "Our admission standards keep rising but student performance is not." (administrator)

Recognizing these frustrations as indicators of cognitive traps is crucial, as addressing them is essential for students to embark on a transformative educational journey that extends beyond the confines of academia and prepares them for success in work and life. Let us seize the opportunity to break free from these traps, fostering an environment where students can thrive, educators can guide, and stakeholders can witness the true power of education to shape lives and futures. Together, we can create an educational experience that transcends expectations, empowering students to embrace their full potential and embark on a path of lifelong learning and growth.

8

THE ACADEMIC MYOPIA TRAP

When I was about 11 years old, my friend Ronnie had a lifechanging event. Growing up in Jacksonville, Florida, Ronnie and I were inseparable, often found hanging out on the block together. Throughout elementary school, we had a customary habit of sitting in the back of the class. So when we entered sixth grade, it was only natural for us to secure our usual seats at the rear of the room. We had a tendency to joke around a bit during class, but we also made sure to do our work. Whenever the teacher posed a question related to the content on the board at the front, we were always prepared with an answer. It might have been a fabrication at times, but it was at least relevant.

One particular day, the teacher called upon Ronnie to read a segment of text displayed on the board. After staring at the board, squinting his eyes, Ronnie shocked both the teacher and me by refusing to read it. Sensing trouble for Ronnie, I quickly intervened and offered to read it in his place.

After class, I couldn't resist asking Ronnie why he had declined to read when the teacher asked. He simply replied that he didn't feel like reading. However, this wasn't an isolated incident; Ronnie refused to read on a few other occasions as well. His refusal to read became a significant point of contention between him and the teacher.

Eventually, the teacher requested Ronnie to stay after class for a conversation. Curiosity got the better of me, so I discreetly eavesdropped on their discussion while standing outside the classroom door. I hoped to hear the teacher reprimand Ronnie, so I could tease him later. As the conversation unfolded, Ronnie initially evaded the teacher's inquiries about his recent negative behavior. However, when pressed further, Ronnie's

DOI: 10.4324/9781003447252-11

eyes welled up with tears as he explained to the teacher that his eyes hurt whenever he tried to read the board.

The teacher inquired about the duration of this problem, to which Ronnie revealed that it had started the year before, back in fifth grade. Remarkably, he had managed to avoid trouble by finding ways around reading. The teacher recognized Ronnie as a proficient reader who had not caused any serious issues in her class. Understanding the situation, she recommended that Ronnie see an eye doctor.

The following week, Ronnie returned to school wearing eyeglasses. I couldn't resist teasing him, telling him he looked like a nerd, and we both shared a laugh. However, from that day forward, Ronnie encountered no difficulties in reading the board. He had been diagnosed with myopia, commonly known as "nearsightedness." The eyeglasses corrected his vision problem, so Ronnie stopped being a problem.

When I held the position of learning center director at Lenoir-Rhyne University, the nursing students had a distinct reputation for their late-night study sessions. The imminent nursing exams would invariably lead them to claim ownership of the study lab rooms. These rooms, with their expansive floor-to-ceiling whiteboards spanning 20 feet high, were their sanctuary. The students relished the opportunity to fill these boards with meticulously color-coded notes.

Once their notes and knowledge were transcribed onto the boards, they would rotate from room to room, attempting to commit every piece of information to memory. Some employed visualization techniques, closing their eyes as they walked and testing their ability to mentally pinpoint the location of information on the boards. The idea behind this method was to enable them to mentally "locate" the necessary information during exams. Others relied on recalling items based on the colors in which they were displayed. The colors served as mental markers, allowing them to mentally sort and retrieve information when confronted with specific test questions. These tactics had proven effective in their academic success throughout their school years.

Since my office was situated in the same building, I would often bring treats for the students and decorate the room with encouraging messages. When the students asked for my opinion on their efforts, I would often tell them that even if they were able to recall every single item on the boards accurately during their tests, their scores would likely not exceed a C. They scoffed at my response, but I knew I was right.

My predictions that their performance would fall short of their expectations often came true. However, I wasn't relying on psychic abilities; instead, I was observing their work through the lens of research that suggested students who employ shallow thinking skills on complex cognitive tests tend to struggle to achieve higher than a C (Flippo & Caverly, 2009).

By the time students reach college, they may already be programmed for superficial thinking. They may have developed an academic value system that prioritizes achieving grades over genuinely understanding the material. This perspective renders them susceptible to what I call "academic myopia."

Academic myopia is akin to nearsightedness. It occurs when students become excessively fixated on the daily content presented in their courses, without considering the deeper underlying concepts. By adopting a different approach, students can build a foundation of conceptual knowledge atop their accumulated factual knowledge. Unfortunately, students suffering from academic myopia fail to construct knowledge in this manner. Instead, they perceive isolated facts as endpoints rather than opportunities for further exploration.

Academic myopia represents a lack of perspective stemming from poor learning practices. As demonstrated earlier in the functional traps section, Students' perspectives on academic work are shaped by their approach to learning. Recall that Each student's approach reflects their vison about what constitutes learning, both within themselves and in others (Entwistle N., 2000). Students can choose to operate from either a surface, deep or strategic vision. Although we delved into this concept more extensively in the Functional Traps section, let's revisit it briefly here.

Students and educators perceive various aspects of learning environments and academic work through one of three distinct lenses: surface, deep, or strategic/achieving approaches to (Biggs, 1987, Entwistle N., 1983, 1991, 2000, Marton F., 1976, Marton F. D., 1993, Saljo, 1979). Those adopting a surface approach view learning as a laborious task of collecting facts to pass tests. On the other hand, students operating from a deep approach seek to understand information in a connected and integrated manner. They believe that knowledge should not only be retrievable but also meaningful and applicable. These students go beyond mere memorization; they synthesize and integrate information (Nelson, 2008). Students employing a strategic approach toggle between surface and deep approaches based on their perceived value of the course. They adopt a deep approach for courses they consider essential, such as those within their major, and a surface approach for courses they deem less important, such as electives.

Students afflicted by academic myopia perceive learning predominantly through a surface lens. Overwhelmed by the sheer volume of content they must absorb, they employ a range of practices and sequences solely focused on memorization. Their studying objective is to cram as much information into their minds as possible, ensuring it remains intact until they are assessed on it.

Academic myopia confines students to a narrow, superficial range of options, rendering them unable to recognize what is truly significant and essential. They place more value on what they perceive their teachers expect than on trusting their own critical thinking abilities (Flippo & Caverly, 2009). I witnessed this scenario unfold among a group of students at McDowell County High School in North Carolina during the fall of 2014. After experiencing deeper thinking and learning through the use of the ThinkWell-LearnWell Diagram (a tool we will explore later in this section), they deliberately reverted back to memorization because they believed it was the skill their teachers desired.

For instance, Isabella had conditioned herself to extract specific information from the literature books she read. This information primarily revolved around the main characters, plot, themes, and settings. Her sole purpose in reading was to identify and gather these elements of the stories as accurately as possible. While this information was helpful, it remained shallow compared to what she could have extracted. Isabella had devised tactics to operationalize her shallow reading approach, employing a story chart to record these items as she read. If she read five different short stories, she would manage her work by creating mental tables, resembling Table 8.1.

Isabella attributed her newfound success and improved understanding to the ThinkWell-LearnWell Diagram. By adopting a deeper thinking approach, she began uncovering what she described as "different" elements within the stories she read. When I probed further, she elaborated on how she started noticing meaning in the colors, settings, names, and word choices used by the authors. She discovered patterns that transcended individual stories and began to contemplate the ideas presented by the authors, seeing their manifestations in the real world.

Recognizing that these insights were a direct result of her ehnaced qualitative thinking about the stories, I encouraged Isabella to share her newfound understanding during her next class. I anticipated her eagerness to enlighten her classmates, but she hesitated, feeling embarrassed and concerned about derailing the class. As someone with experience in college settings, I initially

TABLE 8.1 Isabella's Story Chart

	Main Characters	*Plot*	*Theme*	*Setting*
Story Title (1)				
Story Title (2)				
Story Title (3)				
Story Title (4)				
Story Title (5)				

struggled to understand her hesitation. I was certain her teachers would welcome her contributions to the class discussions with open arms.

Eventually, Isabella mustered the courage to share a fraction of her insights with her class. To her surprise and delight, her contributions completely transformed the class dynamic. Her teacher was astonished by her profound understanding, while her classmates wondered if they had read the same material. Initially, Isabella felt a sense of unease as her classmates responded to her in this new light, but soon she found herself being regarded as the "smart one" among her peers.

Habitual Thinking

Isabella's journey out of the academic myopia trap highlighted the power of deep thinking and the transformative nature of embracing meaningful concepts. However, her initial resistance to this shift in thinking revealed a deeply ingrained habit loop that kept her trapped in shallow thinking patterns. This loop, depicted in Figure 8.1, exemplifies the habitual nature of cognitive traps. To understand how cognitive traps like academic myopia develop, it's important to explore the four phases that gradually shape students' thinking patterns over their academic lifetimes.

How Cognitive Traps Develop

Cognitive traps, such as academic myopia, are not innate conditions but gradually develop over students' academic lifetimes. The cognitive skills utilized by students during their K–12 years have a lasting impact, becoming deeply ingrained and operating unconsciously by the time they reach

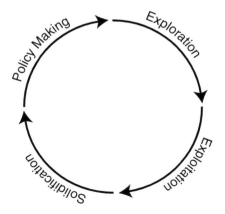

FIGURE 8.1   Shallowing-thinking habit loop.

college. This habituation of thinking occurs through four distinct phases, which we will now explore.

Phase 1: Exploration

When students begin a course, they are uncertain about the expectations. Within this setting, habit-based thinking begins to emerge as students navigate the initial ambiguity (Graybiel, The Basal Ganglia and Chunking of Action Repertoires, 1998). During this exploration phase, students engage in a trial-and-error process, utilizing a range of thinking skills and complex cognitive functions such as analysis, evaluation, decision-making, and meaning-making (Graybiel, Habits, Rituals, and the Evaluative Brain, 2008). Their brains actively seek the most effective skills to accomplish the tasks at hand.

Phase 2: Exploitation

Once students achieve success using their cognitive skills, they transition to the exploitation phase. Positive feedback, good grades, and recognition from educators and peers reinforce their skill utilization. As the brain perceives these rewards, it becomes more efficient in employing the skills, reducing the conscious effort required for thinking (Foerde & Shohamy, 2011). Dopamine, a hormone associated with motivation and reward, plays a pivotal role in reinforcing this behavior. The brain consolidates the intellectual behaviors employed during the exploration phase through a process known as chunking (Graybiel, The Basal Ganglia and Chunking of Action Repertoires, 1998), forming the foundation for habit formation.

Phase 3: Solidification

The brain seeks efficiency by minimizing effort and seamlessly matching the required mental skills with the given tasks. Rather than going through the exploration and exploitation phases each time, the brain automates the activation of the chunked skills without the students' conscious awareness. This leads to the solidification phase, where habits become deeply ingrained within the brain's structures. The chunking process, while powerful, deceives students into believing they have control over their thinking, when in reality, their thinking has become habitual (Graybiel, Habits, Rituals, and the Evaluative Brain, 2008). It involves a shift from a normal action-outcome (A-O) pattern of thinking to a stimulus-response (S-R) pattern. In the A-O sequence, students deliberately engage in thinking to achieve a specific future outcome by selecting the appropriate skill. However, as thinking becomes habitual, students unknowingly transition to a stimulus-response system where their thinking skills are automatically activated in response to stimuli, no longer driven by explicit outcomes. This shift can lead to complex behavioral patterns based on learned responses (Chersi, Mirolli, Pezzulo, & Baldassarre, 2005, p. 212), resulting in a focus on memorization.

This shift to the S-R system explains why nursing students continue to rely on memorization tactics, even when memory assessment is not the primary focus. Despite recognizing the limited usefulness of memorization, students find themselves unable to switch their thinking approach. This phenomenon is known as *reward devaluation*, where students continue to "perform behaviors repeatedly, on cue, even if the value of the reward to be received is reduced so that it is no longer rewarding" (Graybiel, 2008, p. 363). In academic contexts, this explains why students persist in applying the same thinking behaviors, even if they lead to poor grades. The literature on habit formation suggests that students are internally rewarded cognitively and neurochemically, even when external rewards such as grades decrease in value.

Phase 4: Policy-Making

As the habit becomes established, students develop an academic policy that codifies the habit. Importantly, this entire process occurs unconsciously, rendering students unaware and powerless to change it. For instance, Jay's reliance on memorization skills earned him success in his Western History course during his first quiz. Despite consciously studying, Jay's memorization skills kicked in automatically, resulting in positive outcomes. Jay, logically linking his success to his study methods, unknowingly sets a personal academic work policy for future Western History assignments. Jay's policy would sound something like this: "Whenever I must do work in Western History, I will use flashcards for studying because they work well."

Within this policy, the memorization thinking skills become embedded, shaping Jay's academic work not only in Western History but also across his college career.

Understanding the gradual development of cognitive traps sheds light on the subconscious nature of these habits. Awareness of these processes is crucial for facilitating change, as students cannot alter something they are unaware of.

Now, let's explore a strategy to liberate students from academic myopia.

Academic Myopia Rescue Tactics

If you've ever played golf on dormant Bermuda grass during mild winters in the Carolinas, you may have experienced the challenge of finding your ball on overcast days. The ball tends to blend in with the tan-ish grass color, making it difficult to locate. Seasoned golfers in the area have developed a tactic to overcome this myopia when driving the ball with long clubs. Instead of fixating on the exact location of where their ball was hit, they choose a distinct raised object in the approximate area as a reference point. This allows them to navigate the vicinity and eventually pinpoint the ball's precise location. This simple technique of contextualizing the ball has saved golfers from losing both money and their sanity by avoiding lost balls in the middle of fairways.

Similarly, educators can employ a contextualization tactic to help students break free from academic myopia. Like golfers, we need to teach students how to contextualize specific course content. This involves guiding students to hold both the focused content and the broader conceptual context in their minds simultaneously. By training their minds to work with the content and concepts together, students can make meaningful connections that foster deep learning.

Teaching the Three "Cs" of Academic Work

Dr. Winkler had grown tired of his students' constant requests for study guides before tests. Despite his initial resistance, he reluctantly began providing them. However, even with study guides, his students still complained about confusing tests. Frustrated, Dr. Winkler sought a better solution.

To understand his students' challenges, Dr. Winkler started meeting with them individually to discuss their experiences in class and on tests. During these conversations, he noticed that struggling students focused solely on memorizing content. They had a superficial grasp of specific information, like key terms, but lacked a deeper conceptual understanding. Realizing this, Dr. Winkler decided to help his students by teaching them how to separate and integrate the three layers of knowledge. Using a visual representation similar to Figure 8.2, he showed them that they were only engaging with one level and emphasized the need for more mental work to fully comprehend the material. He inspired them by promising that understanding the three Cs of academic work would make learning more rewarding and improve their grades.

Recognizing that the issue was cognitive in nature, Dr. Winkler understood that addressing these academic challenges required a metacognitive approach. While many educators perceive metacognition as "thinking about thinking," its true power and utility encompass much more. Metacognition involves learners' awareness of their internal processes, states, and conditions as they engage with information and tasks in their learning environments (Hennessey, 1999, Kuhn, 2004, Martinez, 2006). As students interact with

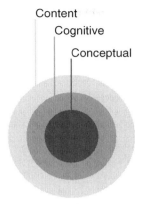

Content

Cognitive

Conceptual

The **content layer** consists of the information that is used to communicate academic concepts.

The **cognitive layer** includes the mental skills that are used to transform content into conceptual products.

The **conceptual layer** consists of the core idea of what's in educators' and students' minds.

FIGURE 8.2 The three Cs of academic work.

Content + Cognition = Conceptual Knowledge

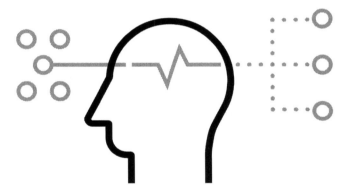

FIGURE 8.3 A formula I have used to promote metacognitive thinking.

content, they must purposefully employ their thinking skills (cognition) to transform their conceptual understanding. This transformation is a vital aspect of the work students must undertake. The relationship between content, cognition, and conceptual knowledge is depicted in Figure 8.3.

Academic work involves the manipulation of external information, such as theories, principles, and formulas, into conceptual knowledge using internal mental forces. This process requires metacognition, as students must manage their cognitive processes while interacting with the content. Through this interaction, students develop conceptual knowledge that serves as a lens for understanding information and the world. Understanding this,

Dr. Winkler took the following steps to free his students from academic myopia traps.

Step 1: Introduce the general idea. Dr. Winkler recognized that his class was hesitant about deviating from the usual course material. To convince them of its value, he explained that understanding the three elements of academic work—the three Cs—could lead to studying less, learning more, and achieving better grades.

Dr. Winkler began by introducing the content layer of learning. He explained that it consists of the raw information conveyed through instruction or obtained from external resources, such as PowerPoint slides, class notes, and highlighted material in books. Separating content as a distinct ingredient in academic work, he emphasized that capturing content is only one part of the process. To truly understand the concepts expressed in the content and their connections, students need to engage with it using both their cognitive and metacognitive skills.

Acknowledging the work students were already doing, Dr. Winkler highlighted the additional mental work required as a natural extension of their current efforts.

To empower his students further, Dr. Winkler explained the cognitive layer, which represents the thinking element of academic work. He introduced Bloom's Higher Thinking Skills as a classification used by educators to describe various thinking skills, including remembering, understanding, applying, analyzing, evaluating, and creating. He emphasized that the level of knowledge produced depends on the thinking skills employed while interacting with the content. Students nodded in agreement, realizing their focus on memorization and superficial understanding.

Dr. Winkler encouraged students to use a range of thinking skills, explaining how each skill contributes to different levels of learning. He maintained a non-threatening, persuasive tone and avoided jargon, ensuring his students understood the transformative effect of thinking on content. With this, he transitioned to the conceptual layer, the innermost element of academic work, comprising the abstract ideas that the content builds upon.

To help students appreciate conceptual knowledge, Dr. Winkler used reliability and validity as examples. He pointed out that their shallow understanding of these concepts, as evidenced by their notes, limited their learning potential. He highlighted the cognitive power they possess to change how they learn such concepts.

Dr. Winkler concluded his introduction of the three Cs by connecting them to previously discussed material, activating students' metacognitive reflective memory skills. He ended on an optimistic note, empowering students with the belief that they have the ability to transform their learning and improve their performance.

FIGURE 8.4   A basic image of a pickup truck.

Step 2: Use a concrete example to solidify new knowledge. The next objective is to help students associate their fragile understanding with a tangible artifact (Figure 8.4).

Dr. Winkler put a picture of a truck on the screen and instructed his students to write down statements that described the image *without writing or saying what it was*. After viewing the students' responses, he organized them in the following manner:

- It has two doors./It has four tires./It's shaped like a box.
- It is used to transport people or things.
- It is like a car, but bigger./It's not a plane, boat, or train.

Dr. Winkler utilized the example of the truck to demonstrate how the interplay between content and cognition aids in grasping concepts. He explicitly explained this interplay to his students, highlighting that none of the words used in their statements directly expressed what the object was. Instead, the content served as tools to generate a mental conception of the object, in this case, a truck. The mental image of a truck represented the abstract idea that was manifested in their minds.

He prompted the students to imagine a scenario where they had focused solely on learning the content without connecting it to the image of a truck. If they were then tested on their conceptual understanding, they would likely perform poorly, despite memorizing the words verbatim. This highlighted the difference between merely knowing the content and truly understanding the concept.

Dr. Winkler acknowledged that his students tended to learn the content but struggled to grasp the underlying concepts. They became fixated on the content covered in class without allowing their minds to fully process it. To address this issue, he emphasized the role of cognition in the knowledge transformation process and its significance in academic work.

Using the class's statements about the truck, Dr. Winkler drew attention to the transformative role that cognition plays in learning. He categorized the statements into different modes of thought, with each line representing a specific level of thinking. The first line described the object's features, the second line addressed its use, and the third line distinguished it from similar objects. He explained that each level of thinking enhanced their capacity to mentally represent the image and improved learning by clarifying their understanding of the object. The interactions between content and cognition were the factors that allowed them to grasp that the object represented a truck.

While the roles of the three Cs (content, cognition, and concept) become clearer when using physical examples like a truck, applying them to abstract course material presents a greater challenge.

Step 3: Use the practical example as a springboard for the academic application. Dr. Winkler employed the same process to demonstrate how the three Cs apply in academic contexts. He presented Table 8.2, focusing on the concepts of reliability and validity.

Dr. Winkler explained that students could have used various levels of thinking skills to interact with these terms, which would have determined the depth of their learning. He listed the different types of mental work associated with each level of interaction, as shown in the table.

As the students examined the table, one student admitted that she usually relied on remembering because it was what she had in her notes. Another student noticed that the analyzing and evaluating questions resembled the more challenging exam questions. A third student asked if they could retake the test.

Dr. Winkler was pleased to see that his students grasped the concept of the three Cs. The classroom atmosphere was charged with excitement, and the students were eager to apply their newfound knowledge. The strategy was successfully motivating them to improve their work.

TABLE 8.2 Reliability and Validity Thinking Mode Grid

Remembering	What is the definition of reliability? What is the definition of validity?
Understanding	Why are reliability and validity important to understanding scientific experiments?
Applying	How do reliability and validity work?
Analyzing	How is reliability distinct from validity? How do they work together?
Evaluating	Which is the best to use in a particular study?
Creating	How would I test the reliability and validity of an instrument?

Step 4: Take some responsibility for the current state of performance. Dr. Winkler acknowledged that he could assist his students in improving their work. He committed to being more explicit and intentional in communicating the cognitive requirements. This step was crucial as it shifted the dynamics of the relationship, making students more receptive to making changes when they believed the system would change as well.

Step 5: Have students immediately apply their new knowledge and skills. Dr. Winkler informed the class that he would return their tests but instead of retaking them, he asked them to identify the levels of thinking involved in each question. He also requested that they write a statement comparing how they previously thought about the material before taking the test to their current understanding. One student humorously commented, "Oh, you want us to analyze our test questions," while another asked jokingly, "Are you going to have us evaluate our analysis next?"

Dr. Winkler laughed, pleased with his students' grasp of the three Cs and their willingness to embrace the challenge of using a broader range of thinking skills in their academic work.

While some educators might consider this instructional detour a waste of time, superficially believing they don't have time for metacognitive work, they would be overlooking a valuable opportunity to free their students from academic myopia traps. Dr. Winkler's deviation from the routine instructional path proved to be a powerful educational moment. His students gained a fresh perspective on academic work, transcending academic myopia and becoming independent learners.

By implementing these steps, Dr. Winkler effectively transformed his students' understanding of academic work, empowering them to engage in more effective and efficient learning processes.

Keys to Success

To replicate Dr. Winkler's effective approach, remember the following guidelines as you follow the steps he used:

1 Select a concise section of your instructional content, whether it's from your notes, PowerPoint slides, a story, math book, or textbook. Choose a manageable portion that can serve as a focused example.
2 Maintain an encouraging tone throughout your instruction. Instead of framing students as deficient, emphasize that their academic processing is a work in progress and has room for growth. This perspective fosters a positive learning environment.
3 Engage students in metacognitive conversations, which are powerful dialogs that shift the focus from the content itself to how students interact

with the content. These conversations highlight the learning process and aim to increase students' awareness of their cognitive abilities to shape how information is transformed.

Engaging in metacognitive conversations can be challenging for educators who are not fully familiar with the construct. In the next chapter, you will learn how to develop students' metacognitive competence gradually over a few class sessions. You will discover how to utilize the ThinkWell-LearnWell Diagram as a metacognitive roadmap to empower students to become more independent learners, enabling students to overcome cognitive challenges related to *far transfer traps*.

Assessment Questions and Exercises for Addressing Academic Myopia

Here are some assessment questions and exercises that you can use to assess whether your students are trapped by academic myopia:

1 Do students primarily focus on memorizing and regurgitating facts without truly understanding the underlying concepts?
2 Are students more concerned with acquiring information for exams rather than developing a genuine curiosity and interest in the subject matter?
3 Do students struggle to apply their knowledge to real-world situations or make connections across different topics within the course?
4 Are students overly reliant on provided study materials (e.g., lecture slides, textbook summaries) without considering the concepts, theories or principles underlying the content?
5 Can your students provide evidence that they are expanding on the daily content that you provide them?

Exercises to Free Students from Academic Myopia

1 **Basic Conceptual Log:** Encourage students to use this tool, located in the Appendix (You can obtain the appendix and additional supporting materials at the following online location: http://www.routledge. com/9781642672893) to chart how their conceptual knowledge develops over time. create concept maps or mind maps that illustrate the relationships between different topics or concepts within the course. This exercise helps them visualize connections and identify overarching themes, promoting a deeper understanding.

2 **Key Relationships Map:** Help students activate your learning outcomes and break free from academic myopia by using this tool, located in the Appendix (You can obtain the appendix and additional supporting materials at the following online location: http://www.routledge.com/9781642672893), to make critical connections that will build strong foundational knowledge for your course and beyond. This exercise cultivates critical thinking, communication skills, and the ability to see beyond surface-level information.

3 **Reflective Writing:** Assign regular reflective writing exercises where students can articulate their understanding, insights, and questions about the course material. This practice promotes metacognition, allowing students to identify gaps in their understanding and develop strategies for deeper learning.

By using these assessment questions and incorporating these exercises into your instruction, you can identify students trapped in academic myopia and provide opportunities for them to break free from limited perspectives, develop effective thinking skills, and engage in deeper learning.

9
FAR TRANSFER TRAP

Imagine encountering someone who aspires to become a professional pianist. This individual informs you that they follow a rigorous daily practice routine, investing countless hours to refine their piano skills. Curious about their approach, you inquire about their practice methods, only to be met with an unexpected response: "I spend four to five hours rollerblading every day!" The incongruity between rollerblading and piano playing skills leaves you perplexed, as if you missed the punchline of a joke. It is evident that the skills acquired through rollerblading cannot possibly prepare them to become a professional pianist. In academic terms, these two skills lack transferability, rendering the rollerblading skills irrelevant to the goal of becoming a professional pianist.

In the example I just provided, the error in the young lady's thinking is evident. However, students often make a similar thinking error when they study. They employ cognitive skills during their study sessions that do not align with the skills their teachers will assess, leading them into what I refer to as far transfer traps.

Transfer of Learning

Transfer of learning resides between the realms of academic myopia (discussed in the previous chapter) and pseudowork (explored in the next chapter). When students concentrate solely on the content of a course without attempting to grasp the underlying concepts, they inadvertently engage in shallow mental processes. These processes rely on memory-based functions like acquisition, storage, organization, and recall. However, when faced with assessments and

DOI: 10.4324/9781003447252-12

tasks that demand a more sophisticated understanding of the subject matter, students realize that their study methods have been insufficient.

Following disappointing test results, students may seek guidance from their teachers, academic coaches, or tutors to enhance their performance. Unfortunately, if these individuals fail to recognize the role of transfer of learning in students' academic lives, they may misconstrue the situation. They might mistakenly attribute students' failures to specific study techniques they deem ineffective, their perceived inability to manage time effectively, or even their presumed inherent limitations. However, viewing students' struggles through the lens of transfer of learning enables us to identify the cognitive trap ensnaring them.

Transfer of learning, as described by Perkins (1992), refers to the degree of alignment between the skills students employ in one context and those required in a different context. Whether knowledge transfers lies at the heart of various academic levels. For instance, when we contemplate whether undergraduate education adequately prepares students for post-graduate pursuits, we are essentially considering transfer. When designing 200-level courses to equip students for 300-level courses, our aim is to foster positive transfer. And when we teach students material over weeks and subsequently evaluate their comprehension, we seek to determine the extent to which transfer has occurred.

Moreover, transfer of learning extends beyond academia and permeates our daily lives. When a child practices dribbling a basketball at the park, they hope their dribbling skills will transfer to the next pick-up game or their upcoming school match. Similarly, as you engage with this book, you anticipate (and I sincerely hope) that the insights you gain will transfer to various facets of your life.

Researchers have identified two types of transfer: near and far (Entwistle N. J., 2001, Entwistle N., 2000, Nelson, 2008). Near transfer occurs when the skills employed in one context align with those required in a different context. It serves as a positive affirmation of students' learning, transpiring when the skills used to acquire knowledge correspond to the skills assessed in a given context. Conversely, far transfer arises when the skills from one context fail to match those needed in another. These experiences are negative and undermine students' learning. Far transfer scenarios frequently contribute to unexpected underperformance. For example, consider the following homework question: "What are Darwin's four postulates that lead to natural selection?" If students rely solely on memorization skills to address the question and the test primarily evaluates their accurate recall of Darwin's postulates, they will likely fare well. This represents a near transfer experience, where the skills employed during studying align with the skills assessed in the test context. Figure 9.1 illustrates what near transfer looks like.

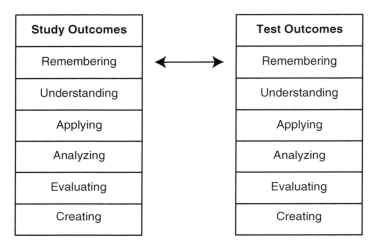

FIGURE 9.1 Near transfer.

As educators, you can identify when students are engaging in near transfer by observing their excitement during an exam. Their external enthusiasm provides a clear indication that the knowledge they have acquired aligns with the knowledge being assessed. Upon closer examination, we recognize that the skills they utilized to generate this knowledge correspond to the skills being evaluated.

However, far transfer experiences take center stage in this chapter. They occur when students utilize a different set of thinking skills to learn the material than the thinking skills that are evaluated. Let's consider an example: imagine our students, who relied on memorization skills to learn Darwin's four postulates, are faced with the following question: "Use Darwin's four postulates to explain how a pesticide-resistance gene might spread in a population of planthoppers living on soybeans." In that moment on the exam, the students would feel that all-too-familiar sinking feeling in their gut (Lightner, 2008). They are experiencing far transfer, realizing that their efforts in studying are not yielding the desired results. They may read the question repeatedly, searching their memory bank for answers, and their gaze may shift to their teacher with tears or frustration in their eyes. The thought bubble above their heads might convey a sense of defeat: "Oh $#!T!".

Similarly, during the virtual learning year of the pandemic, I unfortunately witnessed far transfer experiences draining the enthusiasm from my son. At one point, his class was assigned the classic Edgar Allan Poe poem "The Raven." He read the poem multiple times, but he had never been taught how to analyze poetry. Although he could recall many lines from the poem, when his teacher asked for a deeper analysis of the poem's symbols and imagery, he found himself completely at a loss. He felt as if he had never read the poem at all, despite his repeated readings. He was trapped in a far transfer experience, as the memorization skills he employed to comprehend "The Raven" did not align with the analytical skills his teacher expected.

Farther Is Harder

Figure 9.2 depicts the *Transfer of Learning Grid*. It emphasizes the increasing difficulty and ineffectiveness of study efforts as the skills used in one context increasingly move farther away from the skills assessed in exams. It illustrates how students often find themselves trapped in far transfer situations, where the skills employed during studying do not align with those evaluated in tests and tasks. As a result, students fail to benefit from their studying efforts and experience growing frustration towards themselves and/or their teachers.

Research indicates that the greater the disparity between the skills used while studying and those assessed in exams, the more challenging the task becomes (Perkins, 1992). As the assessed outcomes require more advanced cognitive abilities than the memorization-based skills typically employed during studying, the transfer experience becomes more distant, resulting in a misalignment between the produced outcomes and the ones being assessed.

The first frame illustrates near transfer, where students' mental efforts to memorize the material align with the memory-based skills assessed by educators. The solid, straight, black line represents productive learning, leading to a positive transfer experience. For example, if a student named Jessie studies the principles of public speaking using her memorization skills, and the test assesses her ability to recall and articulate those principles, she will find it easy and experience a positive near transfer. This ease stems from her studying with the same skills that are being evaluated.

The second frame portrays a close far transfer scenario, indicated by the solid crooked line, symbolizing partially productive learning. The mental work of memorization falls just short of the level of understanding assessed by the educator. Since the two types of mental work are closely related, students may experience some positive transfer effects, although not fully benefiting from their efforts.

In this situation, Jessie may face questions that require her to go beyond mere recall and explain the importance of applying the principles of public speaking. Having only utilized her memorization skills, she may attempt to answer by providing additional details about each principle. While this may demonstrate her knowledge of the principles, it does not reflect a genuine

FAR TRANSFER

Study Outcomes	Test Outcomes
Remembering	Remembering
Understanding	Understanding
Applying	Applying
Analyzing	Analyzing
Evaluating	Evaluating
Creating	Creating

VERY FAR TRANSFER

Study Outcomes	Test Outcomes
Remembering	Remembering
Understanding	Understanding
Applying	Applying
Analyzing	Analyzing
Evaluating	Evaluating
Creating	Creating

IMPOSSIBLY FAR TRANSFER

Study Outcomes	Test Outcomes
Remembering	Remembering
Understanding	Understanding
Applying	Applying
Analyzing	Analyzing
Evaluating	Evaluating
Creating	Creating

NEAR TRANSFER

Study Outcomes	Test Outcomes
Remembering	Remembering
Understanding	Understanding
Applying	Applying
Analyzing	Analyzing
Evaluating	Evaluating
Creating	Creating

CLOSE FAR TRANSFER

Study Outcomes	Test Outcomes
Remembering	Remembering
Understanding	Understanding
Applying	Applying
Analyzing	Analyzing
Evaluating	Evaluating
Creating	Creating

SLIGHTLY FAR TRANSFER

Study Outcomes	Test Outcomes
Remembering	Remembering
Understanding	Understanding
Applying	Applying
Analyzing	Analyzing
Evaluating	Evaluating
Creating	Creating

FIGURE 9.2 Transfer of learning grid.

understanding. Nonetheless, since remembering and understanding involve similar mental qualities, Jessie may partially benefit from her studying. This section of the exam may prove challenging for her, and she may feel dissatisfied with her response.

The third frame represents a slightly farther transfer scenario, with a crooked and disconnected line. This indicates that the memorization skills students employed during studying are insufficient compared to the application skills being assessed. In such cases, students may realize their inadequate grasp of the material but mistakenly believe that investing more time in studying will solve the problem.

This part of the test may require Jessie to provide examples of public speaking principles in use. If the examples closely resemble those covered in class or from assigned texts, Jessie will find some alignment between her mental work and the requirements of this section. However, if the examples involve applying the principles to speeches from different genres, contexts, or eras, there is only a 50% chance her knowledge will successfully transfer. Jessie will perceive this section as "hard" because she must engage in more demanding cognitive work during the exam than she did during preparation. Consequently, she may run out of time or simply give up.

The fourth frame depicts the far transfer situation commonly encountered by college students. The crooked and more disconnected line indicates that the memorization skills used for studying are qualitatively different from the analytical skills assessed by the educator. In this case, students perceive little connection between the knowledge they have acquired and the level of knowledge being evaluated, resulting in a highly negative transfer experience.

At this point, Jessie becomes unsure of her performance. Although she felt confident at the beginning of the test, she now realizes that this section requires students to compare how different speakers utilized the principles in their speeches. Having only memorized the principles, she acknowledges her lack of preparedness for such questions. Frustration sets in, and she may even feel that her professor is intentionally trying to deceive her or that she received the wrong test. This experience not only constitutes a negative transfer but also a distressing one.

The fifth frame accentuates the widening gap in far transfer. The increasingly crooked and disconnected line illustrates that the memorization skills provide no preparation for the higher-level evaluative skills being assessed. Mentally exhausted from the previous section, Jessie hopes to bounce back. She has invested ample time studying and preparing for the exam. However, she has not felt confident in her responses since the first segment, and matters only worsen as the transfer distance increases.

The subsequent set of questions delves deeper into comparing speakers, requiring Jessie to rank each speaker's effectiveness in using the principles. As she reads these questions, a feeling of unease creeps into her stomach. Frustration and disappointment manifest as somatic sensations. The stark contrast between the work she did and the work demanded in that moment leads her to contemplate feigning illness to escape the exam, recognizing that an incomplete grade would be preferable to the outcome she anticipates.

The sixth frame illustrates an impossibly far transfer gap. The work done at the remembering level bears no resemblance to the creative skills sought by the evaluator. Instead of faking an illness, Jessie decides to complete the exam. However, upon encountering the task of writing a short speech that integrates each public speaking principle, she breaks down and starts sobbing. She feels angry with herself for wastefully spending so much time studying ineffectively, and she harbors resentment toward her teacher for posing (in her view) unfair questions. Jessie's experience mirrors that of my son. They believed their studying had adequately prepared them, but relying on incorrect cognitive skills ensnared them in far transfer traps.

Differentiating Transition Traps from a Lack of Effort

Before we look at strategies to liberate students from far transfer traps, it is crucial to distinguish between two types of academic situations that students encounter: type I and type II problems.

Type I Problems

Type I problems primarily stem from a lack of effort, where students exhibit a consistent disregard for studying. They frequently skip classes, neglect to engage in studying, and lack seriousness in their approach. These problems solely pertain to issues of effort and necessitate a behavioral approach, which falls beyond the scope of this book. However, it is important to note that not all students struggling with type I problems can be simply dismissed because students in the later stages of type II problems often display characteristics resembling type I behaviors.

Type II Problems

Type II problems involve students who diligently apply themselves to their academic work but fail to achieve satisfactory results. These students are likely ensnared in far transfer traps and can be referred to as pseudoworkers (a topic covered in the subsequent chapter). Although they invest considerable time and effort into their work, their metrics for success are misguided. When assessing your class, regardless of its size, it may seem that many students fall into the category of type I problems. However, Kathleen Gabriel cautions against hasty judgments. In her book *Teaching Unprepared Students* (Gabriel, 2008), she reflects on students who struggle academically, stating that some have "given up on the idea of academic success because of frustration and prior failures" (p. 15). She further notes, "Nearly every one of these students wanted to do well, but after so much failure, some had written off all hope" (p. 16). These observations serve as a constant reminder that the apathy exhibited by students may actually be a psychological defense mechanism masking their inability to meet the required expectations. It can be presumed that the majority of students encountered will fall into the category of type II problems. Keep in mind that being unprepared for college-level academic work doesn't mean students are incapable of the work.

Solutions for type II problems must go beyond simply urging students to work harder or manage their time better, which are commonly provided advice by faculty to struggling students. Instead, educators must assist students in aligning their thinking with the tasks at hand. One effective approach to steer students away from far transfer traps is to help them avoid confusion regarding desired outcomes. We will discuss a plan to achieve this objective in the following section.

Strategy for Avoiding Far Transfer Traps

Often, educators unknowingly create circumstances that lead students into transfer traps. When educators fail to communicate their academic tasks with precision, students can misinterpret the intended outcomes. This misinterpretation of their educators' cognitive expectations results in the adoption of inappropriate thinking skills during studying, which is the root cause of far transfer traps. Over the years, the students I have worked with have developed the perfect term to describe this predicament: *outcome confusion*.

Outcome confusion occurs when students misjudge the expected outcomes of their academic work. When the required modes of thinking are unclear, students are left to navigate blindly. By "blindly," I mean they lack the cognitive guidance necessary to purposefully direct their thinking. My initial realization of this phenomenon came while observing students in group study sessions. As they debated which topics and content were essential versus tangential, I questioned the metrics guiding their decision-making process. When I asked if they were aware of their course outcomes, the typical response was no. These interactions made it evident that these students had no clear understanding of what was expected of them regarding the content, apart from attempting to memorize as much as possible. When students lack awareness of the outcomes they will be assessed on, their studying becomes akin to stumbling around in the dark. However, educators have the power to design and structure their courses in ways that mitigate outcome confusion.

To illustrate, let's consider the case of Dr. Ferguson, who dedicated a significant portion of her chemistry course to exploring different types of chemical reactions. As she presented numerous examples of reactions involving various chemical substances, students diligently transcribed each reaction, believing they would encounter them again on the upcoming unit exam. Driven by the students' compliance and their meticulous note-taking, Dr. Ferguson remained oblivious to the fact that her students were copying the reactions with the expectation of straightforward recall-based questions. However, when the exam demanded their ability to predict reactions resulting from entirely different combinations of substances, the students were ill-prepared for such complex creative thinking.

Unbeknownst to Dr. Ferguson, she had inadvertently created an environment of outcome confusion. The manner in which she delivered the material during class signaled to her students that basic recall skills would suffice. Yet, she evaluated them on their predictive abilities, which require high-level skills such as synthesis, analysis, evaluation, and creation. This disparity in depth left her students perplexed and subjected them to negative transfer in which the skills they employed would not adequately prepare them for the test, regardless of how much they studied.

Upon learning about the unintended consequences of her teaching approach, Dr. Ferguson utilized Figure 9.3, the *ThinkWell-LearnWell Diagram*, as a tool to prevent outcome confusion in her future courses.

The ThinkWell-LearnWell Diagram (TLD) serves as a metacognitive tool that aids educators and students in liberating themselves from far transfer traps by mitigating outcome confusion. This diagram effectively integrates crucial elements of metacognitive regulation, including planning, monitoring, evaluating, and valuating academic work. Each of the four columns within the diagram corresponds to a distinct aspect of the learning regulation process.

The initial column, labeled "Metacognitive Learning Goals," encompasses embedded statements or questions that drive learners' engagement with the content. These thought-provoking inquiries automatically initiate the planning phase of metacognitive regulation.

The second column presents "Bloom's Higher Order Thinking Skills," a widely recognized hierarchy of cognitive abilities. However, it organizes these skills in a top-to-bottom arrangement, with the least complex skills

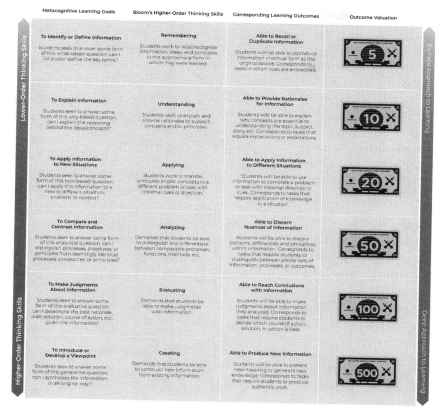

Metacognitive Learning Goals	Bloom's Higher-Order Thinking Skills	Corresponding Learning Outcomes	Outcome Valuation
To Identify or Define Information — Students seek to answer some form of this what-based question: can I list and/or define the key terms?	**Remembering** — Students work to recall/recognize information, ideas, and principles in the approximate form in which they were learned.	**Able to Recall or Duplicate Information** — Students will be able to reproduce information in similar form as the original source. Corresponds to tasks in which cues are embedded.	5
To Explain Information — Students seek to answer some form of this why-based question: can I explain the reasoning behind the ideas/concepts?	**Understanding** — Students work to explain and provide rationales to support concepts and/or principles.	**Able to Provide Rationales for Information** — Students will be able to explain why concepts are essential to understanding the topic, subject, story, etc. Corresponds to tasks that require explanations or elaborations.	10
To Apply Information to New Situations — Students seek to answer some form of this how-based question: can I apply this information to a new or different situation, problem or context?	**Applying** — Students work to transfer principles and/or concepts to a different problem or task with minimal cues or direction.	**Able to Apply Information to Different Situations** — Students will be able to use information to complete a problem or task with minimal direction or cues. Corresponds to tasks that require application of knowledge to a situation.	20
To Compare and Contrast Information — Students seek to answer some form of this analytical question: can I distinguish processes, predures, or principles from seemingly identical processes, procedures, or principles?	**Analyzing** — Demands that students be able to distinguish and differentiate between comparable processes, functions, methods, etc.	**Able to Discern Nuances of Information** — Students will be able to discern patterns, differences, and similarities within information. Corresponds to tasks that require students to distinguish between similar sets of information, processes, or outcomes.	50
To Make Judgments About Information — Students seek to answer some form of this evaluative question: can I determine the best rationale, plan, solution, course of action, etc. given the information?	**Evaluating** — Demands that students be able to make judgments with information.	**Able to Reach Conclusions with Information** — Students will be able to make judgments about information they analyzed. Corresponds to tasks that require students to decide which course of action, solution, or option is best.	100
To Introduce or Develop a Viewpoint — Students seek to answer some form of this generative question: can I synthesize the information in an original way?	**Creating** — Demands that students be able to construct new information from existing information.	**Able to Produce New Information** — Students will be able to present new meaning or generate new knowledge. Corresponds to tasks that require students to produce authentic work.	500

FIGURE 9.3 The ThinkWell-LearnWell Diagram. This metacognitive tool can be used to help align students' thinking with respective outcomes.

occupying the upper positions and more sophisticated skills positioned towards the bottom. These cognitive skills are the tools students employ to process academic material and necessitate continuous monitoring during their learning journey.

In the third column, titled "Corresponding Learning Outcomes," a comprehensive compilation of outcomes emerges based on the thinking skills employed by students. These outcomes become the focal point of scrutiny during the evaluating phase of academic work.

The fourth column, "Outcome Valuation," assigns value to each level of cognitive performance. By attributing value to distinct types of cognitive activities, students can effectively assess and differentiate various levels of academic work.

Collectively, the columns and rows of the ThinkWell-LearnWell Diagram provide educators and students with a structured framework to orchestrate their learning experiences from the outset of academic work. Furthermore, this diagram empowers them to retrospectively analyze their learning process after producing desired outcomes.

Engineering Learning

Preventing or rescuing students from far transfer situations does not involve simplifying academic work, as this would diminish the value of the academic experience. The key to freeing students from far transfer experiences lies in teaching them to discern and differentiate among various thinking skills. This ability necessitates students' comprehension of the characteristics and nuances associated with each thinking skill.

The engineering-learning tactic serves as a valuable approach in helping students distinguish and navigate each level of cognitive engagement. It encompasses the metacognitive conditions that trigger their thinking, the cognitive skills they activate, the resulting outcomes of those skills, and the corresponding values associated with those outcomes. By incorporating this diagram into their instruction and structuring their courses around it, educators facilitate appropriate student interactions with the course content.

Dr. Ferguson's implementation of the ThinkWell-LearnWell Diagram and the engineering-learning tactic in her large online course involved the following steps:

1 Prior to introducing the diagram, Dr. Ferguson distributed copies to each student and encouraged them to familiarize themselves with the columns and rows before the next class. She emphasized that this tool would enhance their studying efficiency and lead to improved grades.

2 In the subsequent class, Dr. Ferguson guided her students in understanding the horizontal relationships among the columns. She explained that the columns depict the process of transforming abstract metacognitive trigger statements into tangible and measurable work products.

3 Dr. Ferguson then helped her students grasp the vertical relationships among the rows, which represent varying levels of interaction and work products. To solidify the concept, she drew comparisons between different levels of academic work and various jobs that offered different remuneration based on the value of the skills required for each job.

4 Armed with these conceptual understandings and aided by the metaphor as a mental guide, Dr. Ferguson commenced teaching her students how to effectively engineer their own learning processes.

Starting the Metacognitive Lesson

To initiate the lesson, Dr. Ferguson introduced her students to a new concept: kinetic molecular theory. Aware of their initial confusion, she encouraged them to vocalize their thoughts and express the questions arising in their minds. Instantly, numerous students typed, "What is kinetic molecular theory?"

Dr. Ferguson had two objectives in mind: first, she wanted her students to acquire a thorough understanding of the kinetic-molecular theory, as it held crucial significance for her course; secondly, she aimed to equip them with the skills to utilize the TLD as a tool for independent and deeper learning. Directing their attention to the diagram displayed on the screen, she requested the class to identify the metacognitive question that best aligned with their current mode of inquiry. In response, her students pointed to the "first column, first row." Acknowledging their response, Dr. Ferguson marked a checkmark on the left side of the row.

Subsequently, Dr. Ferguson outlined the sequence involved in transforming meta-level questions into academic products, stating,

> Whenever you come across new information, your mind will generate questions about that information. The type of question your mind poses matters because the level of thinking involved determines the thinking skills you employ to mentally process the information. And the skills you utilize in processing this information will determine the depth of your outcomes.

Deliberately explicit in her explanation, she aimed to draw her students' attention to these metacognitive relationships.

Seeking feedback, she inquired if the class understood her explanation. After a brief pause, one confident student expressed that he "kinda" grasped the sequence. Dr. Ferguson encouraged the student to elaborate, assuring him that she would assist in filling any gaps in comprehension. The student accurately stated,

> Well, if you have a question at the top of the diagram in your mind, then you will use thinking skills at that level. And if those skills differ from the ones needed to answer test questions, then we won't perform well on those tests.

Commending the student for his correct answer, Dr. Ferguson added, "Indeed, your work won't transfer to your tests because the skills you employ to study the concept and the skills embedded within the tests are different."

Another student unmuted her microphone and contributed,

This makes a lot of sense. I'm a tennis player, and if I want to enhance my lower body strength in my tennis game, I must practice in ways that target my lower body. It would be illogical for me to focus solely on improving my forehand and backhand muscles and expect that work to somehow enhance my lower body strength. So, if I use thinking skills that differ from those being assessed, I can't expect to possess the same level of knowledge.

Dr. Ferguson's visible smile that stretched across the entire screen conveyed her approval of the analogy.

Continuing to move the dialog forward, Dr. Ferguson aimed to provide her students with an experiential understanding of the mental processes involved as they replaced the metacognitive question with increasingly different levels of thinking skills. She posed the question to the class, "What if we substitute 'what is the kinetic molecular theory?' with 'why is kinetic molecular theory important to understanding gases?'"

One student responded, "Whoa, that's a completely different question. Before, we were merely asking what KMT is, but now we're questioning its significance in relation to something else." Dr. Ferguson directed her cursor to the left side of the second row in the ThinkWell-LearnWell Diagram and stated, "Correct, we're not only posing a different question; we're delving deeper." She then pointed her cursor to the far right side of the second row and remarked, "This question holds a value of $10, whereas the initial question was worth $5."

Dr. Ferguson intentionally emphasized a direct correlation between the quality of questions asked by students and the value of the outcomes they would achieve. She recognized the importance of this connection as students engineered their own learning.

Subsequently, Dr. Ferguson provided further clarity on two vital uses of the diagram. She urged,

This diagram serves as both a thinking crosswalk and a thinking scaffold. As a crosswalk, it unveils the relationships among the implicit questions that emerge in your minds when encountering information (column 1), the thinking skills employed to generate knowledge (column 2), the knowledge you ultimately produce (column 3), and a value system for assessing your cognitive performance (column 4). My goal is to assist you in utilizing this tool as a scaffold to construct outcomes that align with the outcomes I evaluate.

She explained,

> As we've witnessed, your minds are already posing basic questions at the top of the diagram. I want you to realize that by altering the meta-level questions your mind seeks to explore, you can train your mind to ask deeper types of questions. As you pose deeper questions regarding the material, you'll produce more profound and valuable outcomes.

And one student typed in, "And higher test scores!"

Observing that the students had grasped the essence of the lesson, Dr. Ferguson aimed to reinforce it through an assignment. She proceeded by asking the students to center their studying around the following five questions:

1 What is the kinetic molecular theory?
2 Why is the kinetic molecular theory important in comprehending gases?
3 How does the kinetic molecular theory operate?
4 How does the kinetic molecular theory differ from Avogadro's theory (a distinct theory about gases)?
5 What factors contribute to the wider adoption of the kinetic molecular theory compared to Avogadro's theory?

Recognizing that they were not yet prepared to engage with the creating level of thinking, she omitted it from the assignment. She instructed them to utilize the "Linking Thinking and Learning" worksheet (You can obtain the appendix and additional supporting materials at the following online location: http://www.routledge.com/9781642672893) to complete the task. This worksheet prompted students to organize their study around specific metacognitive triggers and make notes on how these triggers influenced their thought processes regarding the content.

In the subsequent class, Dr. Ferguson utilized one of the completed worksheets from the students to guide a class discussion on how they must employ this thinking and approach to academic work throughout her course. She stated,

> The purpose of this exercise is to help you learn how to engineer your learning. By this, I mean you should be able to determine the level of outcomes you wish to achieve before commencing your study. Once you establish that, you can strategically select specific modes of inquiry that stimulate the appropriate thinking skills. Finally, when your minds produce the desired outcome, you can evaluate its value. This process is known as engineering your learning.

After addressing a few questions about the lesson, Dr. Ferguson felt content with the students' level of comprehension.

To assist your students in engineering their learning, you can utilize the ThinkWell-LearnWell Diagram by following the steps outlined below. You and your students can download your personalized, colored copy of the diagram at thelearnwellprojects.com/tools.

Steps of the Engineering Learning Technique

Choose a desired level of outcome and repeat these steps until the technique becomes automatic:

1 Explicitly set the metacognitive trigger in the first column.
2 Activate an appropriate mode of thinking in the second column.
3 Verify the outcome produced by the student in the third column.
4 Ascribe a value to the outcome in the fourth column.

In summary, far transfer traps arise from discrepancies between the mental skills employed by students to learn content and the mental skills educators assess. When these traps remain unaddressed, they undermine both the instruction provided by educators and the academic work of students. However, when educators and students fulfill their respective roles, they can evade or overcome transfer traps. By being intentional about using the appropriate cognitive language to formulate course learning outcomes and explicitly communicating those outcomes, we can assist students in avoiding transfer traps. Furthermore, equipping students with tools such as the ThinkWell-LearnWell Diagram and tactics like the engineering-learning tactic enables them to steer clear of outcome confusion and engage in positive near transfer learning experiences.

Assessment Questions to Identify Far Transfer Traps

1 What is far transfer in the context of learning?
2 Can you explain the difference between near transfer and far transfer?
3 Describe a scenario where students might encounter a far transfer trap.
4 How does outcome confusion contribute to far transfer traps?
5 Provide an example of outcome confusion in academic work.
6 What role does metacognition play in avoiding far transfer traps?
7 How can the ThinkWell-LearnWell Diagram help students recognize and overcome far transfer traps?

Exercises to Identify and Overcome Far Transfer Traps

8 **Create Metacognitive Learning Outcomes:** The best way to avoid far transfer trap and related experiences, such as outcome confusion is to craft metacognitive learning outcomes and use them as recommended in the Structural Traps section.

9 **Comparison and Contrast Exercise:** Provide students with two related concepts or theories and ask them to compare and contrast their key principles, applications, and implications. Evaluate their ability to differentiate between similar concepts and identify transferable knowledge.

10 **Collaborative Problem-Solving:** Form groups and assign complex problems that require students to work together and draw on their diverse knowledge and skills. Assess their ability to effectively communicate, integrate different perspectives, and transfer knowledge across domains.

11 **Scaffolded Learning:** Design learning activities that gradually increase in complexity, building on previously acquired knowledge. Provide clear guidance and support to help students recognize and apply their existing knowledge to new situations.

12 **Metacognitive Reflection:** Prompt students to regularly reflect on their thinking processes and learning strategies. Encourage them to identify transferable skills and develop metacognitive awareness to avoid outcome confusion.

By incorporating these assessment questions and exercises into your work with students, you can assess their understanding of far transfer traps and provide opportunities to both identify and overcome them in your class and others.

10

PSEUDOWORK COGNITIVE TRAP

As mentioned previously, I enjoy observing students while they are study-ing. I often strike up a conversation about how they are doing their work. On one particular occasion, as I was setting up for one of my Transforming Students into Great Learners workshops, I noticed an adult student deeply engrossed in studying at the library across from the workshop room. What caught my attention was the absence of a computer on her table, as she only had a textbook, pens, pencils, and a stack of college-ruled paper. Intrigued, I couldn't resist the urge to inquire about her studying methods and what she was studying.

As the student rose to stretch, I took the opportunity to introduce myself and strike up a conversation. She introduced herself as Mary and informed me that she was preparing for her pharmacology nursing exam. Mary revealed that her academic standing in the nursing program hinged on passing this crucial class, and she needed a minimum score of 87 to remain enrolled.

With my curiosity piqued, I asked Mary what she was doing to achieve the required grade. Mary disclosed that she was rewriting the entire text-book. Initially, I believed she might be exaggerating, so I requested to take a look at her notes and the book. To my astonishment, I observed that Mary had devoted countless hours to meticulously transcribing the text-book word for word. When I questioned her motive behind this approach, she explained,

> The topics covered in class never seem to appear on the tests, so I assumed the information must come from the book. I decided to rewrite

DOI: 10.4324/9781003447252-13

the entire book, thinking that the process would help solidify everything in my mind.

Encountering a student who was painstakingly transcribing an extensive textbook was a first for me. Regrettably, it was not the first time I had witnessed students engaging in what I call "pseudowork."

What Is Pseudowork?

In a nutshell, pseudowork is futile labor that fails to produce the desired outcomes. Within academia, pseudowork refers to tasks that promise favorable results but ultimately deceive and disappoint. Norman and Jenson shed light on the origins of the "pseudo" in pseudowork, stating,

> The prefix pseudo comes from the Greek term *pseudos*, meaning lie or deception. You put it at the beginning of a word to signal that what comes after is not really what it appears to be. A pseudonym, therefore, is not a real name. Pseudoscience is not real science.
>
> *(Nørmark, 2021)*

This breakdown of the term "pseudo" by the authors offers valuable insight. Pseudowork presents itself as genuine work, resembling authentic efforts, but in reality, it is deceptive. This can be likened to students who spend hours studying, only to realize that the knowledge they acquired does not align with what is needed. Pseudowork misleads individuals into believing they are making progress, when in truth, their actions will prove to be wasteful. Consider the hardworking nursing students who diligently filled massive whiteboards with information. They may have felt productive as the hours ticked by, but they were ultimately deceived when their efforts failed to yield good grades. They had fallen into the trap of pseudowork.

Pseudowork holds allure because it offers both internal and external benefits to those engaged in it. Mary's extensive hours of transcribing served as a means of stress relief, occupying her time and mental space that would have otherwise been consumed by worries about her performance. Mary found false security in her pseudowork, believing that her relentless efforts would guarantee the desired grade. Hard work felt like progress to her, and it appeared as dedication to others. Students and educators praised Mary's work ethic and commitment, unknowingly affirming her as a serious-minded student. Unfortunately, these observers did not realize they were applauding someone deceived by pseudowork.

Cal Newport, a Georgetown professor and author of *How to Become a Straight-A Student*, highlights the prevalence of pseudowork in academic settings. He suggests that most students are unaware they are engaging in pseudowork, as it is the norm and how their peers operate (Newport, 2007, p. 15). Through years of observing students' academic work, I came to realize that their study efforts were well-intentioned but ultimately futile, regardless of their capabilities or the amount of time they invested. From a conventional perspective, their actions seemed sensible, but when viewed through the lens of pseudowork, they were entirely senseless. These students lacked direction, rendering their studying nothing more than aimless activity.

Students who fall into the trap of pseudowork engage in actions that are simultaneously rational and unreasonable. Rationality focuses on immediate or local purposes, addressing a situation narrowly. Reason, however, takes a broader view, considering the global context. For example, a farmer sowing spinach seeds is acting rationally within the scope of their profession. Yet, if that farmer were to plant spinach seeds during the scorching heat of a 90-degree summer, their behavior would be considered unreasonable. While the act of sowing spinach seeds remains the same, the context (the "why" and "when") is crucial. Spinach seeds must be planted during cooler months to yield a harvest. By sowing seeds at a time that will not result in a successful harvest, the farmer is engaging in pseudowork. Their rational actions become unreasonable, and their labor becomes in vain.

Students resemble the farmer in this analogy. Their actions are rational on the surface. "I need to study for my test," they reason. Thus, they read through their notes, write on whiteboards, solve problems, transcribe texts, and so forth. However, because they lack explicit goals and defined outcomes for their efforts, their work lacks context and fails to produce the desired academic results. Their labor becomes pseudowork—a heap of wasted activity. It is important to note that all students engage in pseudowork at times, but some become serial pseudoworkers, falling victim to its enticing allure.

I have long been convinced that pseudowork is the most common obstacle to academic achievement. Unfortunately, hardworking students often believe they do not require assistance, as they perceive it as something reserved for lazy students. To attract students caught in the trap of pseudowork, I have always advised my clients to use its ensnarement as bait. Students are drawn to messages such as, "Do you feel like your grades don't improve, regardless of how much you study?" Pseudoworkers resist traditional forms of academic support, such as tutoring, supplemental instruction, and academic coaching, because they see themselves as "smart, good students." Their self-image is not entirely incorrect. They resist assistance because the pseudowork they engage in convinces them that success is within reach if they just work a little harder.

When I handed Mary a flyer for the workshop series, she immediately agreed to attend. Throughout the series, I learned a great deal about students' perspectives on academic work, including Mary's experiences during her time in the program.

Students engage in various forms of pseudowork. They study extensive lists of information, discuss course content with peers, and work through problem sets together. Each of these actions is considered good practice, displaying rationality. However, what transforms them into pseudowork is the absence of clarity regarding how these actions fit into an overall strategy for achieving the desired outcomes in their respective courses. Without this clarity, their efforts become unreasonable and are destined to be in vain. When students toil in vain, the consequences are felt by everyone—students, educators, and the entire institution.

Educators and institutions unknowingly steer students toward pseudowork by emphasizing the measurement of academic work in terms of time. If you have ever advised students to study a certain number of hours for each hour of class, you unintentionally set them up for the pseudowork trap. Institutions that employ time as a metric for academic success through study hall programs or conditional admittance programs, without providing clear guidance on the academic outcomes students must achieve, inadvertently encourage pseudowork. It's not that these statements or initiatives are inherently wrong; rather, they are based on a flawed equation of academic work.

Studying Harder Is Not Studying Smarter

Cal Newport conducted interviews with straight-A students for his book and found that they spent less time studying compared to their peers who achieved slightly lower grades. These high-performing students emphasized the importance of *efficiency* in college and defined it as "the ability to complete work quickly and with minimal wasted effort" (Newport, 2007, p. 15). Newport developed the Engagement Formula as a guide for students to enhance their academic work:

> The Engagement Formula
> Work accomplished = time spent + intensity

The Engagement Formula

Newport argues that pseudowork arises when students engage in unfocused, low-intensity work, wasting time on activities like mindlessly reviewing notes and reading. According to the Engagement Formula, if students increase their intensity and focus while studying, they can spend less time studying overall. Many educators also operate from this perspective, believing that if students become more actively engaged in their coursework, their frustrations will be resolved. However, solely focusing on intensity and time spent studying can lead students into the pseudowork trap.

While the Engagement Formula has its merits, it overlooks a crucial element of academic work that is necessary to break free from pseudowork. By solely adhering to the Engagement Formula, students are susceptible to cognitive traps as it establishes deceptive metrics for success. Students often measure their progress based on how much time they spend studying and how mentally invested they are in their work. This misguided approach convinces students that working harder, such as studying for longer durations and with greater intensity, is the only solution to their academic challenges. However, as we have seen with Cole and Mary, hard work alone does not guarantee success. Intensity without clarity leads to futile efforts and engages students in pseudowork.

Having observed capable and diligent students over many years, I have discovered a formula that students implicitly follow, which I call the Laborer's Formula:

Laborer's Formula
outputs = studying + time

Laborer's Formula

Operating according to the Laborer's Formula, students confuse outputs with outcomes. Outputs refer to the actions students undertake to achieve desired outcomes. Tasks categorized as studying, such as reading, taking notes, and other similar activities, are considered outputs of academic work. However, outcomes are the mental constructs that outputs are meant to develop. When students' outputs fail to produce the expected outcomes assessed by their educators, they have fallen into pseudowork, regardless of the time and intensity they put into studying.

The Laborer's Formula provides emotional benefits that make it appealing and even addictive to students. Each completed task brings them emotional gratification, with more arduous tasks yielding greater rewards (Foerde & Shohamy, 2011). Mary experienced a sense of mental euphoria as she accumulated her textbook transcriptions, while Cole felt expectant after long hours of studying. The nursing students admired their notes on the whiteboards, congratulating themselves on their outputs. However, when asked outcome-focused questions, they were unable to provide satisfactory answers. As actor Denzel Washington highlighted in his 2015 commencement speech at Dillard University, "Just because you are doing a lot more doesn't mean you are getting a lot done. Don't confuse movement with progress" (Dillard University, 2020). To avoid such confusion, students must adopt a new metacognitive-based formula, which I call the Learner's Formula:

> The Learner's Formula
> productive learning = correct content + appropriate cognition + time

The Learner's Formula

The Learner's Formula emphasizes the understanding of nuanced elements of academic work. Academic success is measured by outcomes, not outputs, and a sequence is involved in achieving these outcomes. Linda Elder and Richard Paul assert that, "If we think well while learning, we learn well. If we think poorly while learning, we learn poorly" (Elder & Paul, 2010, p. 38). Therefore, successful academic outcomes require students to synergize three key elements:

1 Possessing the correct content: Students need to engage with the subject matter that serves as the object of their thinking.
2 Thinking well: Students must employ appropriate cognitive skills while interacting with the content.
3 Investing sufficient time: Learning takes time, but the duration depends on the interplay between cognition and content.

According to Elder and Paul, thinking well is essential for effective learning. To think well, students must apply the appropriate cognitive skills to the correct content for an appropriate period. The Learner's Formula recognizes that cognition and content are the primary factors, with the necessary mental manipulation involved. The time required to achieve successful outcomes varies based on the cognitive complexity and the level of clarity students possess.

For instance, let's consider the example of Jessie from the previous chapter, who was taking a public speaking course. If Jessie knew in advance that her upcoming exam would assess her ability to evaluate the effective use of public speaking principles in different contexts, she would understand the two critical elements of the Learner's Formula: the principles of public speaking as the correct content and the need to engage evaluative thinking to master the material. Time becomes a factor as Jessie deliberately applies evaluative thinking (along with other relevant thinking skills) to process the content until she can mentally represent the principles of public speaking at the desired cognitive level.

By embracing the Learner's Formula, students prioritize outcomes over outputs, recognize the significance of appropriate cognition and content, and understand that time is relative to the other factors. This metacognitive-based approach empowers students to engage in productive learning and avoid the pitfalls of pseudowork.

The Learner's Formula Improves Mental Representations and Academic Outcomes

I refer to this way of interacting with content as the Learner's Formula because it centers academic work around students' mental representations. Mental representation, as defined by (Pitt, 2019), refers to the informational impressions that remain after students have engaged with new information. It is when students experience those "ah-ha" moments during studying and use phrases like "I see" to describe how murky concepts become clear. These moments signify the achievement of mental representations, which align with academic outcomes. Therefore, instead of asking students how much time they spent studying, we should be asking them about the level of mental representation they have achieved. By accurately assessing their mental representations, students can ensure that their study outcomes match their assessment outcomes and effectively avoid pseudowork.

As an example of the impact that using The Learner's Formula can have on students, consider Kristina, a sophomore from Denison University. She described the benefits like this: "It never occurred to me that the way that I was thinking and processing information may not be aligned with my professors' expectations and, therefore, could be making a course more difficult for me than it needs to be." Using the correct formula helped her make straight-line connections between her thinking, her mental products and her professors' expectations.

Implementing the Learner's Formula empowers students to regulate the depth and quality of their mental representations during academic work. This skill is invaluable as it enables them to establish direct connections between their thinking processes, mental outputs, and the expectations of their professors. By eliminating pseudowork, students like Kristina, can learn faster and better by aligning their thinking with their academic goals.

Banishing Pseudowork for Everyone

Pseudowork not only hampers academic progress but also robs students of the joy of learning, as (Ramsden, 2005) highlights. Genuine academic work is accompanied by pleasurable experiences that sustain students and are ultimately rewarded with good grades. Engaging in meaningful academic work allows students to acquire content knowledge and build conceptual understanding. Moreover, it offers invaluable insights into their identities as learners, which can be transferred across different academic contexts.

Although pseudowork is pervasive, it can be addressed with relative ease. Since it stems from the cognitive traps of academic myopia and far transfer, we can build upon the solutions to those traps. To help students escape pseudowork, I propose the following steps, which a large public university on the west coast used to assist their entire first-year class:

Step 1: Create metacognitive learning outcomes (MLOs) by using the Metacognitive Learning Outcome (MLO) Rubric (Figure 10.1). This framework guides the creation of new learning outcomes or the conversion of existing ones into MLOs.

Step 2: Provide students with opportunities to synchronize the various elements of the course. Two exercises, "Cleaning Up the Muddiest Point" and "Metacognitive Minute Paper," can facilitate this step. Allocating just five minutes at the end of class for these exercises can help students avoid hours of pseudowork and reduce the need for instructors to reteach material.

The "Cleaning Up the Muddiest Point" exercise assists students in using their thinking to clarify confusing or under-processed course concepts. You can help students achieve better levels of clarity by asking them to respond to the following three directives.

1 Write down any remaining information that is unclear.
2 Identify the level(s) of thinking you have achieved and the level(s) that are missing.

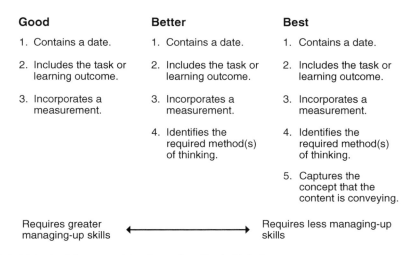

FIGURE 10.1 Metacognitive Learning Goals Rubric.

3 Provide a concise conceptualization of the desired outcome you must produce with the content.

This exercise was adapted from the *Muddiest Point* (Angelo, 1993).

The "Metacognitive Minute Paper" exercise enhances students' capacity for learning by synthesizing content, cognition, and conceptual elements of academic work. Students must answer three questions:

1 What are the most meaningful content items covered in class? (You should consult your notes and/or the professor's presentation.)
2 What mode(s) of thinking is required for that content?
3 What is the desired outcome you need to produce?

This exercise was adapted from the *One-Minute Paper* (Burns, 2013).

Step 3: Help students create and utilize Academic Smart Goals (ASGs) to streamline their academic work (See appendix). When students use ASGs, they effectively manage their workload. If their ASGs fall below the "good" category, they will need to invest more effort in managing their academic tasks due to increased ambiguity. Conversely, when students' ASGs meet all five components of a "best" ASG, they can study with greater clarity and certainty.

Step 4: Implement early and comprehensive assessments. To counteract the tendencies of academic myopia and shallow thinking, it is crucial to assess students as early as possible. But when should this assessment take place? Ideally, it should occur as soon as enough material has been covered or assigned for students to develop a deep understanding. This initial assessment should go beyond surface-level knowledge and require analytical and evaluative thinking. By doing so, both students and instructors can gauge whether students are engaging in the desired levels of thinking. Consider this first assessment as a tool for formative feedback.

As an example of how a resubmission exercise can be used as a formative feedback tool, consider this example from an economics professor. An economics test response might include reflections like:

Upon reviewing the question that asked for a comparison between supply and demand, I realized that my answer was superficial. I merely provided textbook definitions without truly analyzing the concepts. I now understand that the question required a deeper analysis rather than a mere demonstration of familiarity with the terms. In this resubmission, I delved into the shoe market (as I have a keen interest in shoes), and this shift in thinking took me to a whole new level of understanding. Moreover, I found this approach to be more enjoyable.

This step allows educators to ensure that students produce accurate information and, more importantly, employ appropriate cognitive processes.

By engaging in pseudowork, students hinder their ability to reap the rewards of their study efforts. Pseudowork exhausts them on an endless treadmill of busyness and leads faculty to adopt ineffective instructional methods. Regardless of students' capabilities or their dedication to studying, unless they break free from the pseudowork trap, they will miss out on the joys of learning and may jeopardize their academic careers.

Students often employ one of three formulas for their academic work: the Engagement Formula, which increases their involvement but does not prevent pseudowork; the Laborer's Formula, which instills a sense of accomplishment but does not foster effective or productive learning; and the Learner's Formula, which holds the key to liberating students from the pseudowork trap. By utilizing the insights and guidance provided in this chapter and throughout the book, we can collectively banish pseudowork and create a more fruitful academic environment for everyone.

Assessment Questions for Teachers

1 What specific strategies or techniques do you employ to ensure that your academic work is purposeful and not simply an act of busyness?
2 How do you gauge the depth of understanding and engagement your students demonstrate in their assignments? What evidence or indicators do you look for?
3 Can you identify any patterns or behaviors among your students that suggest they may be engaging in pseudowork? If so, what are those indicators and how do you address them?
4 In what ways do you assess the quality of thinking and critical analysis displayed by your students in their academic work? How do you differentiate between genuine understanding and surface-level knowledge?
5 What measures or strategies do you implement to provide constructive feedback to students and guide them away from pseudowork tendencies?

Self-Assessment Questions for Students

1 Do I feel a genuine sense of accomplishment and progress in my academic work, or do I find myself constantly busy without a clear purpose or direction?
2 Am I able to explain the underlying concepts and connections in the topics I study, or do I rely mostly on rote memorization or regurgitation of information?

3 How often do I engage in reflective thinking to evaluate the effectiveness of my study methods and adjust them accordingly? Am I open to adapting my approach when necessary?
4 Do I seek meaningful challenges and opportunities to apply my knowledge in real-world contexts, or do I primarily focus on completing tasks and checking off requirements?
5 Do I actively seek feedback from instructors and peers to improve my understanding and refine my thinking, or do I shy away from critique and prefer to stay within my comfort zone?

Note: These assessment questions provide a fresh set of prompts and activities to assess and address pseudowork tendencies. They aim to stimulate effective thinking, focused learning and the correct learning outcomes.

Conclusion and Call to Action

In our quest to create effective classroom and learning environments, we must navigate the treacherous terrain of cognitive traps that hinder student learning and impede our instructional effectiveness. We must challenge academic myopia by encouraging effective thinking and conceptual understanding. Break free from far transfer traps by designing interdisciplinary and real-world learning opportunities. Banish pseudowork by fostering metacognition and self-assessment. By understanding and addressing these common pitfalls of performance, we can pave the way for transformative learning experiences that allow students to soar and allows us to find greater fulfillment in our roles.

In committing to establishing transition trap-free environments, we will transform our classrooms into vibrant hubs of intellectual growth and genuine engagement. Students will flourish, soaring to new heights of understanding, and we will experience the profound joy of unlocking students' minds. Let us embark on this journey of transformation, dismantling transition traps and shaping a future where learning is truly liberating for all. Our students are counting on us!

EPILOGUE

Now that we have concluded this enlightening journey, we stand on the precipice of a future filled with promise and possibility. I sincerely hope that the vision I presented at the beginning of this book, which envisions a smooth transition from high school to college, where students excel academically, feels more within reach than ever before. With the knowledge and revelations shared within these pages, we are now better equipped to navigate the challenges that hinder our students' progress.

The truth is, our students possess immense potential and readiness when they step foot on campus. Countless hours of dedication invested in their education have honed their skills and shaped their mindsets. They are the cream of the crop, the promising individuals who hold the key to a brighter tomorrow.

However, we must confront the disheartening reality that many of these students falter and fail to graduate. The disconnect between their expected performance and actual outcomes is a puzzle that can leave us questioning their abilities and our own effectiveness as educators. But let us not succumb to despair or blame. Instead, let us embrace a more hopeful reality—one that acknowledges the transitional dilemmas our students face.

This book has unveiled the intricate dynamics between relationships and transitions, shedding light on the traps that ensnare our students. We have explored the Structural Traps, where the influence of the high school classroom hampers their progress. We have delved into the Functional Traps, where their expectations clash with the realities of college-level teaching. And we have exposed the Cognitive Traps, where inadequate mental processes and skills hinder their ability to thrive in the college academic landscape.

By understanding these traps, we have taken the first step toward liberation. We have recognized that our students are not broken or apathetic; they are simply caught between the familiar and the unfamiliar, struggling to adapt to new expectations and demands. Armed with this knowledge, we have the power to transform their experiences and guide them toward success.

It is incumbent upon us, as college educators, to forge a new path forward. We must dismantle the misconceptions and negative narratives that hinder our students' academic achievements. We must create an infrastructure that supports their growth and empowers them to navigate the challenges they encounter.

Throughout this book, we have shared real stories and research, comparing how students leverage their relationships for success in high school versus college. We have discovered the hidden lessons and dysfunctional dynamics that impede their progress. But now, it is time to move beyond identification and focus on solutions.

To break the cycle of low enrollment and financial instability, we must shift our focus from the relentless pursuit of new student recruitment to the crucial task of retaining our current students. This shift is not merely a strategic adjustment, but a transformative step towards ensuring their success and the stability of our institutions.

As a consultant and strategist, I invite you to consider five actionable steps that are entirely within your control, whether you are reading this book alone or with colleagues. These steps should be regarded as guidelines—a roadmap for success that will lead us towards transformative change.

Step 1: Heightened Awareness

The first step on our path to success is heightened awareness. We must recognize that transition traps are not always obvious at first glance. They unfold gradually, often disguising themselves as minor issues within students' control. By cultivating a keen sense of observation, we can detect these traps in their early stages, before they escalate and hinder our students' progress.

Step 2: Early Intervention

Once we identify the signs of transition traps, we must intervene early and decisively. Rather than allowing negative narratives to deflate us, or relying on simplistic solutions or temporary fixes, we must address the root causes—the core transitional problems that hinder our students' academic journey. Through targeted interventions, guidance, and support, we can equip our students with the skills, mindset, and infrastructure they need to flourish.

Step 3: Collaborate with Colleagues

No journey towards success is accomplished in isolation. Transition traps are likely lurking throughout your institution, hampering your colleagues and their students. Find creative ways to share your findings and successes through events, such as lunch and learn sessions, departmental meetings, faculty assembly sessions, and professional development events. Collaborate with support systems, such as the center for teaching and learning, your campus learning center, athletics, and more. By pooling our collective wisdom and experiences, we can develop innovative strategies, interventions, and support systems that address the diverse needs of our students. Through collaboration, we strengthen our ability to guide and empower them towards academic excellence.

Step 4: Activate Students

Students can become effective allies in identifying and dismantling transition traps. Train peer tutors, study hall leaders, resident advisors, student government leaders, student-athlete leaders, and Greek life leaders to support their fellow students. By involving students in the process, we can foster a sense of ownership and empowerment, creating a community that actively works to eradicate transition traps.

Step 5: Broadcast Successes

Since students are likely to suffer from transition traps in silence, blaming themselves for their struggles, it's imperative that you and your allies do all that you can to make them aware that transition traps exist and that there is help for them. Share success stories, showcase the positive impact of interventions, and ensure that the entire campus community is aware of the available resources and support. By amplifying the message that help is available, we can break the stigma surrounding transition traps and encourage students to seek assistance when needed.

As we conclude this chapter, remember that the power to transform lies within our hands. By shining a light on transition traps and actively working to resolve them, we can create an educational landscape where every student thrives. Our dedication and unwavering commitment will open doors to boundless possibilities, allowing our students to rediscover the joy of learning and nurturing a lifelong thirst for knowledge.

Together, let us embark on this transformative mission, dismantling the traps that stifle our students and unlocking the limitless potential that awaits them. The time for action is now, and our students are counting on us to lead the way.

BIBLIOGRAPHY

American Psychological Association. (2021, September 3). *Dictionary.* Retrieved from American Psychological Association: https://dictionary.apa.org/functional-fixedness

Anderson, L., & Krathwohl, D. (2001). *A Taxonomy for Learning, Teaching, and Assessing: A Revision of Bloom's Taxonomy of Educational Objectives.* New York: Longman.

Angel, R., & Merken, S. (2021, May). Assessing TILT in a college classroom. *The National Teaching & Learning Forum, 30,* 1–4.

Angelo, T. A. (1993). *Classroom Assessment Techniques: A Handbook for College Teachers.* San Francisco: Jossey Bass.

Aristotle. (n.d.). De Anima (On the soul). *Classics in the History of Psychology.* Retrieved from https://psychclassics.yorku.ca/Aristotle/De-anima/de-anima3. htm (Original work published ca. 350 BC)

Azevedo, R., & Cromley, J. (2004). Training on self-regulated learning facilitate students' learning with hypermedia? *Journal of Educational Psychology, 96(3),* 523–535.

Baker, L. (2009). Metacognition in comprehension instruction. In S. E. Duffy (Ed.), *Handbook of Research on Reading Comprehension* (pp. 353–374). New York: Routledge.

Barefoot, B. O. (2000). The first-year experience: Are we making it any better? *About Campus, 4,* 12–18.

Barnes, T., Kubota, Y., Hu, D., & Denze, J. (2005). Activity of striatal neurons reflects dynamic encoding and recoding of procedural memories. *Nature, 437(20),* 1158–1161. doi:10.1038/nature04053

Biggs, J. (1987). *Student Approaches to Learning and Studying.* Hawthorn: Australian Council for Educational Research Ltd.

Boud, D., & Falchikov, N. (2006). Aligning assessment with long-term learning. *Assessment & Evaluation in Higher Education, 31(4),* 399–413.

Burns, A. & Burns, S. (2013). One-minute paper: Student perception of learning gains. *College Student Journal, 47*(1), 219–225.

Chersi, F., Mirolli, M., Pezzulo, G., & Baldassarre, G. (2005). A spiking neuron model of the Cortico-Basal Ganglia circuits for goal-directed and habitual action learning. *Neural Networks, 41*, 212–224. doi:10.1016/j.neunet.2012.11.009

Chick, N., & Taylor, K. (2013, March 11). *Making Student Thinking Visible: Metacognitive Practices in the Classroom.* Retrieved June 19, 2018, from Vanderbilt University Center for Teaching: http://cft.vanderbilt.edu/2013/03/making-student-thinking-visible-the-impact-of-metacognitive-practice-in-the-classroom

Clapper, T. (2012, March 7). *Metacognition: Are Your Learners Really Thinking about the Content?* Retrieved from The EvoLLLution: https://evolllution.com/opinions/metacognition-are-your-learners-really-thinking-about-the-content/

Council, C. (2022, November 22). *Nature of Academic Work.* Retrieved from Canadian Association of University Teachers: https://www.caut.ca/about-us/caut-policy/lists/caut-policy-statements/policy-statement-on-the-nature-of-academic-work

Coutinho, S. (2008). Self-efficacy, metacognition, and performance. *North American Journal of Psychology, 10*(1), 165–172.

Dillard University. (2020, December 10). *Dillard University 2015 Commencement Address | Denzel Washington [Video].* Retrieved from YouTube: https://www.youtube.com/watch?v=ROiNPUwg9bQ

Doyle, T. (2008). *Learner-Centered Teaching: Putting the Research on Learning into Practice.* Sterling: Stylus Publishing.

Drexel University. (2021, August 14). *Drexel University School of Education.* Retrieved from Drexel University: https://drexel.edu/soe/resources/student-teaching/advice/how-to-write-a-lesson-plan/

Dunlosky, J., & Metcalfe, J. (2009). *Metacognition.* Thousand Oaks: Sage Publications, Inc.

Efklides, A. (2011). Interactions of metacognition with motivation and affect in self-regulated learning: The MASRL model. *Educational Psychologist, 46*(1), 6–25. doi:10.1080/00461520.2011.538645

Eklund-Myrkog, G. (1997). The influence of the educational context on students nurses' conceptions of learning and approaches to learning. *British Journal of Educational Psychology*, 371–381.

Elder, L., & Paul, R. (2010). Critical thinking: Competency standards essential for the cultivation of intellectual skills, Part 1. *Journal of Developmental Education, 34*(2), 38–39.

Entwistle, N. (1983). *Understanding Student Learning.* New York: Nichols Publishing Company.

Entwistle, N. (1991). Approaches to learning and perceptions of the learning environment. Introduction to the special issue. *Higher Education, 22*(3), 201–204.

Entwistle, N. (2000). Promoting deep learning through teaching and assessment: Conceptual frameworks and educational contexts. *TLRP Conference.* Leicester.

Entwistle, N. J. (1988). Motivational factors in students' approaches to learning. *Learning Strategies and Learning Styles*, 21–51.

Entwistle, N. J. (2001). Conceptions, styles, and approaches within higher education: Analytical abstractions and everyday experience. In R. Sternberg & L.-F. Zhang (Eds.), *Perspectives on Cognitive, Learning and Thinking Styles* (pp. 103–106). New Jersey: Lawrence Erlbaum Associates.

Fitzgerald, M. A. (2004). Making the leap from high school to college: Three new studies about information literacy skills of first-year college students. *Knowledge Quest, 32*(4), 19–24.

Flavell, J. (1976). Metacognitive aspects of problem-solving. In L. B. Resnick (Ed.), *The Nature of Intelligence* (pp. 231–236). Hillsdale, NJ: Erlbaum.

Flavell, J. (1979). Metacognition and cognitive monitoring: A new area of cognitive-developmental inquiry. *American Psychologist, 34*(10), 906–911. doi:10.1037/0003-066X.34.10.906

Flippo, R. F., & Caverly, D. C. (Eds.). (2009). *Handbook of College Reading and Study Strategy Research* (2nd ed.). New York: Routledge.

Foerde, K., & Shohamy, D. (2011). The role of the Basal Ganglia in learning and memory: Insight from Parkinson's disease. *Neurobiology of Learning and Memory, 96*(4), 624–636. doi:10.1016/j.nlm.2011.08.006

Gabriel, K. F. (2008). *Teaching Unprepared Students*. Sterling: Stylus.

Gale, A. (2020, July 15). *Management Today: Championing British Business.* Retrieved from Managementtoday.co.uk: https://www.managementtoday.co.uk/why-amazon-banned-powerpoint/leadership-lessons/article/1689543

Geddes, L. (2022, January 15). *Metacognitive Teaching Tactics - 1-month Check-in.* Retrieved from YouTube: https://www.youtube.com/watch?v=1On7YqpASGs

Grant, W., & McTighe, J. (2001). *Understanding by Design.* Upper Saddle River: Prentice-Hall, Inc.

Graybiel, A. M. (1998). The Basal Ganglia and chunking of action repertoires. *Neurobiology of Learning and Memory, 70*(1–2), 119–136. doi:10.1006/nlme.1998.3843

Graybiel, A. M. (2008). Habits, rituals, and the evaluative brain. *Annual Review of Neuroscience, 38*(1), 359–387. doi:10.1146/annurev.neuro.29.051605.112851

Hacker, D. J., Dunlosky, J., & Graesser C., A. (2009). *Handbook of Metacognition in Education.* New York: Routledge.

Hacker, D. J., Dunlosky, J., & Graesser, A. C. (Eds.). (1998). *Metacognition in Educational Theory and Practice.* Mahwah, NJ: Lawrence Erlbaum Associates, Inc.

Hall, C. W., & Webster, R. E. (2008). Metacognitive and affective factors of college students with and without learning disabilities. *The Journal of Postsecondary Education and Disability, 21*, 32–41.

Hall, N. H. (2004). The role of attributional retraining and elaborative learning in college students' academic development. *The Journal of Social Psychology, 144*(b), 591–612.

Hargrave, A. R. (2015). Learning, instruction, cognition. *The Journal of Experimental Education, 83*(3), 291–318.

Hennessey, M. (1999). Probing the dimensions of metacognition: Implications for conceptual change in teaching-learning. *National Association for Research in Science Teaching.* Paper presented at the National Association for Research in Science Teaching, Boston, MA.

Hofer, B. K., & Pintrich, P. R. (2002). *Personal Epistomology: The Psychology of Beliefs about Knowledge and Knowing.* Mahwah: Lawren Erlbaum Associates, Inc, Publishers.

Hyde, L. (2007). *The Gift: Creativity and the Artist in the Modern World.* New York: Vintage Books.

Hyde, L. W. (2019). *The Gift: How the Creative Spirit Transforms the World.* New York: Random House.

Immediate College Enrollment Rate: NCES. (2022, March 16). Retrieved from National Center for Educational Statistics: https://nces.ed.gov/programs/coe/indicator/cpa

Jones, M. J. (2022, June 8). *Gallup Blog.* Retrieved from Gallup: https://news.gallup.com/opinion/gallup/242441/confidence-higher-education-down-2015.aspx?g_source=link_NEWSV9&g_medium=TOPIC&g_campaign=item_&g_content=Confidence%2520in%2520Higher%2520Education%2520Down%2520Since%25202015

Kelemen, W. (2000). Metamemory cues and monitoring accuracy: Judging what you know and what you will now. *Journal of Educational Psychology, 98*(4), 800–810.

Kuhn, D. & Dean, D. (2004). A bridge between cognitive psychology and educational practice. *Theory into Practice, 43*(4), 268–273. doi:10.1207/s15430421tip4304_4

Lightner, R. B. (2008). Faculty and student attitudes about transfer of learning. *InSight: A Journal of Scholarly Teaching, 3*(1), 58–66.

Locke, T. (2022, Janaury 21). *CNBC News.* Retrieved from cnbc.com: https://www.cnbc.com/2019/10/14/jeff-bezos-this-is-the-smartest-thing-we-ever-did-at-amazon.html

Martinez, M. E. (2006). What is Metacognition? *Phi Delta Kappan, 87*(9), 696–699.

Marton, F. (1976). On qualitative difference in learning: Outcome and process. *British Journal of Educational Research,* 4–11.

Marton, F. D. (1993). Conception of learning. *International Journal of Educational Research, 19*(3), 277–300.

McGuire, S., & McGuire, S. (2015). *Teach Students How to Learn.* Sterling: Stylus.

McTigue, J., & Willis, J. (2019). *Upgrade Your Teaching: Understanding by Design Meets Neuroscience.* Alexandria: ASCD.

Mehta, J., & Fine, S. (2019). *In Search for Deeper Learning: The Quest to Remake the American High School.* Cambridge: Harvard University Press.

Merriam-Webster. (2019, October 21). Retrieved from Typecast: https://www.merriam-webster.com/dictionary/typecast

Moseley, D. B. (2005). *Frameworks for Thinking: A Handbook for Teaching and Learning.* Cambridge: Cambridge University Press.

Moseley, D., Elliott, J., Higgins, S., & Gregson, M. (2005). Thinking skills frameworks for use in education and training. *British Educational Research Journal, 31,* 3, 367–390.

Nørmark, D. (2021). *Pseudowork: How We Ended Up Being Busy and Doing Nothing.* Copenhagen: Glyndendal.

National Research Council. (2000). *How People Learn.* Washington: National Research Council.

Nelson, T. F., Shoup, R., Kuh, G. D., & Schwarz, M. J. (2008). The effects of discipline on deep approaches to student learning and college outcomes. *Springer Sciene and Business Media, 49*(6), 269–494.

Nelson, T. O. (1990). Metamemory: A theoretical framework and new findings. *Psychology of Learning and Motivation, 26,* 125–173.

Newell, S., Robertson, M., Scarbrough, H., & Swan, J. (2002). *Managing Knowledge Work and Innovation* (2nd ed.). London: Red Globe Press.

Newport, C. (2007). *How to Become a Straight-A Student. The unconventional Strategies Real College Students Use to Score High while Studying Less*. New York: Three Rivers Press.

Nicol, D. J.-D. (2006). Formative assessment and self-regulated learning: A model and seven principles of good feedback practice. *Studies in Higher Education, 31*(2), 199–218.

NSSE: National Survey of Student Engagement. (2021, June 12). Retrieved from NSSE: https://nsse.indiana.edu/nsse/

O'Brien, J. M., & Cohen, W. M. (2008). *The Course Syllabus*. San Francisco: Jossey-Bass.

Online Etymology Dictionary/Professor. (2021, July 17). Retrieved from Online Etymology Dictionary: https://www.etymonline.com/word/professor

Organization for Economic Co-operation and Development. (2018). *PISA 2018 Results*. National Center for Education Statistics. https://nces.ed.gov/surveys/pisa/pisa2018/#

Perkins, D. & Salomon, G. (1992). *Transfer of Learning*. Oxford: Pergamon Press.

Piaget, J. (1980). *Adaptation and Intelligence*. Chicago: University of Chicago Press.

Pinker, S. (2015). *The Sense of Style*. New York: Penguin Books.

Pintrich, P. R. (2002). The role of metacognitive knowledge in learning, teaching and assessing. *Theory into Practice, 41*(4), 219–225.

Pitt, D. (2019, August 7). *Mental Representation*. Retrieved from Stanford Encyclopedia of Philosophy: https://plato.stanford.edu/entries/mental-representation/

Projects, T. L. (2022, November 28). *21 Savage Student Learning Tips*. Retrieved from The LearnWell Projects: https://www.youtube.com/watch?v=HjfWvbFU3gI

Ramsden, P. (2005). *Learning to Teach in Higher Education* (2nd ed.). New York: Routledge Falmer.

Rotter, J. B. (1966). Generalized expectancies for internal versus external control of reinforcement. *Psychological Monographs: General and Applied, 80*(1), 1–28.

Saljo, R. (1979). *Learning in the learner's persepctive: Some commonsense conceptions*. Sweden: Reports from the Department of Education.

Schraw, G. C. (2006). Promoting self-regulation in science education: Metacognition as part of a broader perspective on learning. *Research in Science Education, 36*, 111–139.

Snowman, J. (2006). *Psychology Applied to Teaching*. New York: Houghton Mifflin Company.

Tait, K. (2009). Understanding tertiary student learning: Are they independent thinkers or simply consumers and reactors? *International Journal of Teaching and Learning in Higher Education, 21*(1), 97–107.

Tanner, K. D. (2012). Promoting student metacognition. *CBE—Life Sciences Education, 11*(2), 113–120.

Taylor, S. (1999). Better learning through better thinking: Developing students' metacognitive abilities. *Journal of College Reading and Learning, 30*(1), 34–45.

Thaler, H. R., & Sunstein, R. C. (2009). *Nudge: Improving Decisions About Health, Wealth, and Happiness*. New York: Penguin Books.

Tofade, T. E. (2013). Best practice strategies for effective use of questions as a teaching tool. *American Journal of Pharmaceutical Education, 77*(7), 155.

Undergraduate Retention and Graduation Rates: National Center for Educational Statistics. (2022, March 16). Retrieved from National Center for Educational Statistics: https://nces.ed.gov/programs/coe/indicator/ctr

Wikipedia. (2022, February 15). *Free encyclopedia.* Retrieved from Wikipedia, the free encyclopedia: https://en.wikipedia.org/wiki/Time_flies_like_an_arrow;_fruit_flies_like_a_banana

Winkelmes, M.-A. (2013, January). Transparency in learning and teaching. *NEA Higher Education Advocate, 99*(2), 6–9.

Young, A., & Fry, J. D. (2008). Metacognitive awareness and academic achievement in college students. *Journal of the Scholarship of Teaching and Learning, 8*(2), 1–10.

Zaidi, S. M., & Moshin, M. (2013). Locus of control in graduation students. *Internationa Journal of Psychological Research, 6*(1), 15–20.

Zimmerman, B. J., & Schunk, D. H. (2011). Attaining self-regulation: A social cognitive perspective. In P. R. M. Boekaerts (Ed.), *Handbook of Self-Regulation* (pp. 13–39). New York: Routledge/Taylor & Francis Group.

Zohar, A., & Dori, Y. J. (2012). *Metacognition in Science Education.* New York: Springer.

INDEX

Note: **Bold** page numbers refer to tables; *italic* page numbers refer to figures.

Sunstein, C. 4, 5, 7
surface and deep approach 16, 17, 95,
 115, 129
surface vision, of students 113–115,
 117; *vs.* deep vision 111, **112**

teacher-centric approach 95
teacher monitors students' application 45
teachers 1–4, 6–17, 21, 24, 25, 27, 29,
 35–37, 39–47, 49–51, 55–57,
 62, 67, 68–71, 84–88, 90,
 91, 99–101, 104, 105, 107,
 109, 110, 116, 121, 124, 127,
 128, 130, 131, 142–145, 148;
 structural traps affect 30–32;
 undivided labor on 72–74
teaching process 1, 2, 10, 11, 16,
 24, 25, 30, 31, 68, 72, 75,
 76, 89, 90, 92, 95, 97–101,
 103–105, 117, 124, 152, 153;
 responsibility for 5, 7, 12, 23,
 24, 31, 32, 37–38, 47, 48, 68,
 97, 106, 139; three "Cs" of
 academic work 134–139
Teaching Unprepared Students (Gabriel)
 149
test-prep approach 11
Thaler, R. 4, 5, 7
ThinkWell-LearnWell Diagram (TLD)
 130, 140, 150, 152, 154, 156
three "Cs" of academic work 134–139,
 135
360-degree approach 19
timeline of tests 36
time-management skill 81
TLD *see* ThinkWell-LearnWell Diagram
 (TLD)
transfer of learning 21–23, 142–145;
 far transfer (*see* far transfer

traps); near transfer 21–23,
 143–145, *144*; negative transfer
 22, 147, 150; positive transfer
 21, 22, 143, 145, 147
transition traps 1, 5, 7, 14, 15, 25, 37,
 68, 168, 170, 171; lack of effort
 148–149; types of 3–4
Transparency in Learning and Teaching
 (TILT) in Higher Education
 framework 8–9, 49
transparency measures 8
20/80 paradigm trap 97, 100, 101,
 105
type I problems 148
type II problems 149
typecasting educators **106,** 107–109,
 108–109

undivided labor: on students 71–72; on
 teachers 72–74
unwitting learners 3

volume of information 36–37

Washington, D. 162
web of transitional dilemmas 2
Webster, R. E. 21
well-conceived MLOs 57
well-designed structure 28
well-oiled pulley system 40
Winkelmes, M.-A. 8, 49
workspace trap 39–42; in action 62–68;
 assessment 42–43; beginning
 44; college workspace 48–49;
 connect 44; high school
 classroom 43; middle 45–56;
 MLOs 56–62

Young, A. 21

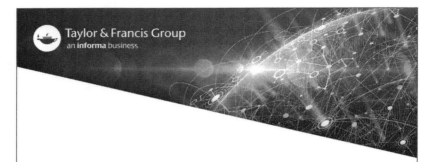

Made in the USA
Coppell, TX
10 September 2024

37032063R00109

Challenging traditional notions about why successful high school graduates struggle in college, this book sheds light on the obstacles that hinder a seamless transition and provides clear guidance on how to overcome them.

Drawing from research and real-life stories of educators and students across a variety of institutions, Geddes illuminates a critical truth: it's the successes students had in high school that work against them in college, not their failure This book explores the hidden structural, functional, and cognitive traps that undermine students' academic work, strain teacher-student relationships, and impose artificial limits on their potential. Armed with formulas for academic success, it provides tools for guiding students towards levels of high performance and supplies teaching methods for how to create an educational environment conducive to success.

Packed with practical advice, actionable steps, and inspiring success stories, this landmark book serves as an invaluable roadmap for college educators seeking to empower their students and revolutionize their institutions.

Leonard Geddes is the founder of The LearnWell Projects, an academic success organization devoted to making learning more visible, manageable, and effective A highly regarded higher education consultant and strategist with 20+ years' experience, he is also the former Associate Dean of Students and Director of th Learning Commons at Lenoir-Rhyne University, USA.

HIGHER EDUCATION

Routledge
Taylor & Francis Group

www.routledge.com

Routledge titles are available as eBook editions in a range of digital formats

CERTIFIED
CARBON
NEUTRAL®
Publication
CarbonNeutral.com

an **informa** bus

ISBN 978-1-642-67289

9 781642 672893